# The Kierkegaard Monograph Series

### edited by
### Alastair McKinnon

# IB OSTENFELD

---

# SØREN KIERKEGAARD'S PSYCHOLOGY

---

---

## translated and edited by Alastair McKinnon

*Wilfrid Laurier University Press*

Translated from
*Søren Kierkegaards Psykologi*
Copyright © 1972 by Rhodos, Copenhagen
Translation copyright © 1978 by Alastair McKinnon
Published by
Wilfrid Laurier University Press
Wilfrid Laurier University
Waterloo, Ontario, Canada
N2L 3C5

Canadian Cataloguing in Publication Data

Ostenfeld, Ib, 1902-
    Søren Kierkegaard's psychology

(Kierkegaard monograph series)

Translation of Søren Kierkegaards psykologi.

ISBN 0-88920-068-8

1. Kierkegaard, Søren, 1813-1855 − Psychology.
I. McKinnon, Alastair, 1925-    II. Title.
III. Series.

B4376.O8213          198'.9          C78-001631-9

Cover design by Mary Wagner

# Acknowledgments

Permission to quote has been kindly granted by the following:

*Søren Kierkegaard: The Journals 1834-54,* trans. by Alexander Dru (1938), by permission of the Oxford University Press.

Søren Kierkegaard, *The Point of View for my Work as an Author,* trans. and ed. by Walter Lowrie (1939), by permission of the Oxford University Press.

*Søren Kierkegaard's Journals and Papers,* vols. 1-6, ed. and trans. by Howard V. Hong and Edna H. Hong (Indiana University Press, 1967-78), reprinted by permission of Indiana University Press.

Søren Kierkegaard, *Concluding Unscientific Postscript,* trans. by David F. Swenson and Walter Lowrie (Princeton University Press, 1941), reprinted by permission of Princeton University Press and the American Scandinavian Foundation.

Søren Kierkegaard, *For Self-Examination and Judge for Yourselves!,* trans. by Walter Lowrie (Princeton University Press, 1944), reprinted by permission of Princeton University Press.

Søren Kierkegaard, *Attack upon "Christendom,"* trans. by Walter Lowrie (Princeton University Press, 1944), reprinted by permission of Princeton University Press.

References to the original Danish *Papirer* (*Pap.*) are to *Søren Kierkegaards Papirer*, ed. by P. A. Heiberg, V. Kuhr, and E. Torsting (Gyldendal, 1909-48). I am grateful to Professor Howard V. Hong for identifying certain of these references.

# Contents

# Translator's Introduction

During the past several years I have been at work on a number of Kierkegaard studies most of which will almost certainly be too long for a paper and too short for a book. During this same period I have also received several Kierkegaard manuscripts from other authors of roughly similar length. It then occurred to me that the obvious solution was to publish these under the general title *The Kierkegaard Monograph Series* and, as this idea met with general approval, I concluded that I should act as Editor. The present volume is the first in this series and more should follow shortly.

The title of this particular book is a literal translation of that of the original Danish and requires a brief explanation. It does not refer to Kierkegaard's psychological theories but instead to his equally interesting and important personal psychology. In fact, it attempts to show that Kierkegaard's life and work can be adequately explained in terms of normal psychology and that, despite the stresses and strains of his environment, he was an essentially healthy and stable individual.

As Dr. Ostenfeld's Introduction shows, Kierkegaard's psychological health has been studied by a number of European scholars over a long period of time. Further, these studies have had considerable influence upon the interpretation of Kierkegaard's thought. Unfortunately, however, virtually none of these studies has thus far been available to the English reader. I am therefore pleased to be able to provide a translation of this balanced and well documented study of this important question and particularly pleased to be able to present it as the first volume in this new series. I believe it to be intrinsically interesting and valuable in and of itself but will be particularly gratified if it helps to discourage the all too common tendency to dodge the challenge implicit in Kierkegaard's works by dismissing him as unbalanced or perhaps even insane. Certainly this work casts serious doubts upon this easy and agreeable assumption.

Note that I have translated *Inderlighed* as *inwardness* and that, with both Kierkegaard and Ostenfeld, I use this term in the sense of fervent religious devotion or intimacy as distinct from psychological introversion or anything of that sort. Note also that I have supplied certain references and biographical information with which the English reader may not be familiar.

I would be less than honest if I did not here confess what until now has been a well kept secret. This book has been translated with a great deal of aid and assistance from the computer. The process by which this was done is described in some detail in a forthcoming issue of *Revue* (Université de Liège) and it seems unnecessary to describe it here. I should however record the fact that this undertaking was originally conceived and begun in 1973 while I was an Honorary Fellow at the Institute for Advanced Studies in the Humanities at the University of Edinburgh, that Mr. Per Bondesen produced the first draft of a translation upon the basis of the original computer output, that Miss Susan Corrente produced a second draft in the summer of 1976, and that I completed the present translation over the Christmas vacation of 1976 using the original text, the computer output, and the two drafts mentioned above. I am, of course, most grateful to both Mr. Bondesen and Miss Corrente for their assistance but assume and accept all responsibility for the present and final form of this translation.

In his Introduction Dr. Ostenfeld graciously thanks me for undertaking to translate his work into English. For my part I should like to thank him for entrusting his work to a wholly inexperienced and untried translator.

This book has been published with the help of a grant from the Canadian Federation for the Humanities, using funds provided by the Social Sciences and Humanities Research Council of Canada. I should like to express my grateful appreciation to both these organizations in this connection.

McGill University                                    Alastair McKinnon
April, 1978

# Author's Introduction

The publication of this work in English provides me with an opportunity to say something about the history of psychological and psychiatric studies of Kierkegaard in and around Denmark.

It should be noted at the outset that psychiatry was not a medical specialty in Denmark until the period 1880 to 1890 and that psychiatric studies of Kierkegaard are themselves quite recent. Indeed, the first author to study Kierkegaard from a medical point of view was P. A. Heiberg, who was himself a physician and whose views are mentioned in the conclusion of chapter 1 of this work. In the twentieth century the famous German psychiatrist, E. Kretschmer, diagnosed Kierkegaard as a leptosomatic type with schizothymic characteristics, an interpretation which Hj. Helweg opposed in his large monograph of 1933 in which he argued that Kierkegaard showed manic-depressive aberrations. This theory was in turn attacked from two different points of view. In 1942 the Swedish scholar John Bjørkhem repeated Kretschmer's views in a small and not very penetrating book. Helweg's other opponents have mainly used normal psychology as a means of understanding Kierkegaard. These include Vodskov, the Danish theologian Ammundsen who wrote a very useful work on Kierkegaard's youth in 1912, the physician Carl Jørgensen who wrote a good monograph in 1964, and myself.

There are, of course, many problems concerning Kierkegaard's psychology. These include his own ambiguous views, his penetrating dialectical manner, his frequent use of pseudonyms, his indirect and tenuous relations with his surroundings, and so on. Some have been inclined to see these as evidence of an inner schism in his nature and have undertaken to explain them in terms of the "deep causes" postulated by psychiatry. But in fact one should use the less radical method of beginning with normal explanations and turning to pathological ones only when the former prove inadequate. Unfortunately, many writers in this field have not been sufficiently cautious and have advanced pathological explanations even when common-sense ones appear to be sufficient.

In connection with the publication of this English translation I should like to make the following brief remarks.

The present version contains some material, especially pages 5-7 and 56-65, not found in the original but provided and intended for inclusion in this translation.

I wish to express my great thanks to Professor Alastair McKinnon of McGill University. I am greatly indebted to him for his initiative in translating this work and for the honour he has done me in doing so.

Summer, 1977                                                    Ib Ostenfeld, M.D.

# Preface

It has long been my wish to conclude my work on Søren Kier-kegaard by sketching the portrait of this unusually gifted but also very complicated person which I have created for myself over the years and which I have attempted to present in my earlier papers "Om Angst-Begrebet i *Begrebet Angest*" ["Dread" in *The Concept of Dread*] (1933) and in "Poul Kierkegaard. En Skæbne" [Poul Kierke-gaard: His Fate] (1957). I was given an opportunity to do so during the winter of 1971, when I was invited by the Søren Kierkegaard Society to lecture on Kierekgaard's psychology.

The present study, a slightly expanded version of that lecture, is an investigation of the basic ideas and personality characteristics that are essential to an understanding of Kierkegaard and that he himself most emphasized. It is particularly concerned with the questions whether, given the unique conditions of his life, he was psychically normal and whether there were disorders in his character, something of which I am myself rather sceptical. All the important points and conclusions appeared in the original lecture and I have added only such material as seemed necessary for a written presentation.

I have been occupied with Kierkegaard's personality and his strange family for more than a generation and in my account I shall try to give a kind of defence of this extraordinary man, who is usually considered by psychiatrists to be mentally ill. It seems to me that there is need for a fresh, professional look at this delicate problem.

Though I dare not call myself a Kierkegaard expert, I still feel that, in my own way, I am an old Kierkegaardian.

Summer, 1971                                          Ib Ostenfeld, M.D.
                                                     Copenhagen (Denmark)

# 1

# Melancholy

It has often been claimed, with weighty and apparently convincing arguments, that the most important feature in Søren Kierkegaard's temperament was a melancholy or depression, a pre-disposition that he inherited from his family, that he carried with him throughout his life, and that coloured both his published writings and private papers. Such a distinguished scholar as Hj. Helweg, late Professor of Psychiatry at Copenhagen University, has strongly advocated this view. We shall investigate this claim by considering the most pertinent quotations from Kierkegaard's own hand in order to discover what he himself meant by the expression melancholy. Here, as always, we must be aware of the fact that Kierkegaard employs his own terminology, uses words in his own way, and gives them meanings quite different from their contemporary ones. I have italicized those parts that are especially important for a proper understanding of his meaning.

"My life *began* without immediateness, with a terrible melancholy, *in its earliest youth* deranged in its very deepest foundations, a melancholy which threw me for a time into sin and debauchery and yet (humanly speaking) almost more insane that guilty" (*Dru*, 754. *Pap*. VIII,1 A 650). "If my melancholy has misled me, then it must have been by making me consider as guilt and sins what perhaps was only an unhappy suffering or temptation" (my translation. *Pap*. IX A 488). "(Merciful God, my father too *was terribly unjust to me* in his melancholy—an old man who put the whole weight of his melancholy upon a child, *not to speak of something even more frightful,* and yet for all that he was the best of fathers)" (*Dru,* 681. *Pap.* VIII,1 A 177). This thought is repeated in the *Papers:* "A relationship between father and son, where the son secretly discovers everything after, and yet dares not acknowledge it. The father is a respectable man, severe and God-fearing, only once in a state of intoxication he lets drop a few words which *hint at the worst.* Otherwise the son does not discover what it is and never dares ask his father or others" (*Dru,* 503. *Pap.*V A 108).

The *Papers* are particularly rich in analysis of the so-called melancholy, which again and again is related to the father's influence. "When melancholy as he was, he saw me melancholy, his prayer to me was: Be sure that you really love Jesus Christ" (*Dru,* 773. *Pap.* IX A 68). Again ". . . humanly speaking, you can say that it has been my misfortune that I was brought up so strictly in Christianity. *From the earliest times,* I have been in *the power of an original melancholy.* Had I been brought up *in a more ordinary way,* then *it is not likely that I would have become so melancholy* . . . But familiar as I was from the beginning with the Christian conception of the thorn in the flesh, with the idea that such things are a very part of being Christian, I considered that nothing could be done about it and in any case accepted my melancholy as part of this entire view" (my translation. Cf. *Hong* 6, 6603. *Pap.* X,2 A 619). Earlier in the *Papers* we find a reference to the familiar theme of father and son. The father stands before his son and says: ". . . you go around in a quiet despair. . . . But father and son were, perhaps, two of the most melancholy men in the memory of man. . . . And the father believed that he was the cause of the son's melancholy, and the son believed that he was the cause of the father's melancholy, and so they never discussed it . . ." (*Dru,* 483. Cf. *Hong* 1, 745. *Pap.* V A 33).

Again in *The Point of View,* published posthumously but written in 1848, Kierkegaard returns to the theme which, as a basic motive in his life, always held his thought captive: "*From a child* I was under the sway of a prodigious melancholy, the depth of which finds its only adequate measure in the equally prodigious dexterity I possessed of hiding it under an apparent gaiety and *joie de vivre.* . . . Already in my earliest chilhood *I broke down* under the grave impression which the melancholy old man who laid it upon me himself sank under. A child—what a crazy thing!—travestied as an old man" (*Point,* p. 76).

"... [O]ne can do what one will ... only one thing excepted ... the throwing off of the melancholy from which and from its attendant suffering I was never entirely free even for a day" (ibid., p.78). And again, "*As far back as I can remember* I was in agreement with myself about one thing, that for me there was no comfort or help to be looked for in others. ... *my thought* was, *as the expression of a melancholy love for men*, to be helpful for them, to find comfort for them ..." (ibid., p. 79).

In the *Papers*, Volume V, there are a number of allusions to the problems of the melancholy mind. "Many a young life has been corrupted because rigorism made it (sexuality) melancholy and sinful." "In all my melancholy I was a passionate mind—my *melancholy is really the form of my passion*." "Since I had never lived before, I assumed that living in this way with a thorn in the flesh (i.e., with my melancholy) was part of the pleasure." "All melancholy is laconic, but it also has its own peculiar pithiness." And, finally, the famous note in the diary on August 16, 1847: "(I shall) not begin on a new book, but try to understand myself, and *really think out the idea of my melancholy together with God here and now*. This is how I must get rid of my melancholy and bring Christianity closer to me. Hitherto I have defended myself against my melancholy with intellectual work which keeps it away—... " (*Dru*, 694. *Pap*. VIII, 1 A 250).

In my own earlier little work on *The Concept of Dread* (1933) I noted that Kierkegaard speaks of his melancholy as "*different from* [*his*] *father's melancholy*." In his own case it is dialectical, a phenomenon of reflection, something to which he "*can relate himself*." Furthermore, though he cannot on his own work himself free of it, *his poetic imagination can* even *display itself* in defiance of it; indeed, it can even *blossom in spite of it*. In fact, he is even able to use this melancholy for his own purposes. He regards it as being as much a consequence of external fate as of guilt. In one place he admits that this melancholy can make him *proud*, that he feels a certain satisfaction in that sovereign loneliness it has produced within him. Summarizing these matters, I wrote then that such melancholy is not something which is added early or late in life but is instead a part of one's innermost predispositions. In fact, the melancholy was Kierkegaard himself, his original temperament enhanced and set in relief by his father's suggestive influence.

In Kierkegaard's self-analyses there is not a single feature which reminds one in the least of the depression associated with and due to manic depression. It must be emphasized that what Kierkegaard here calls melancholy is a fact of his nature *from the beginning*, something impressed on the child Søren by the depressed mood hovering over the home and nourished every day by his dominating father's real and genuine suffering. His father's strong and violent peasant mind was deeply rooted in West Jutland and, feeding on its own sickness, always hung over the home like a threatening black cloud.

What Kierkegaard called his melancholy was the resonance of mood created by the upbringing he received from his sick father. The father grafted his melancholy onto his son and thus attained such a hold over him that Søren was unable to escape his influence. On the contrary he became so swallowed up by his father's thoughts and ideas that it required the work of a lifetime to set himself even partially free. Gradually he was able to voice his criticism but now his love and reverence held him in a new way and this tension remained as a basic problem throughout his life. Kierkegaard was not genetically destined to become melancholy like his brother Peter Christian. He was, however, deeply affected by living with his disturbed father and his mood throughout life was dictated by this traumatic experience. A helpless, impressionable, lateborn child, he was affected by a sensitivity which bound him in a firm dependency relationship to his father.

The quotations cited fully demonstrate that the melancholy of the father and the son were of very different kinds. The son preserves a wondering and analytic attitude toward his father's ways, but he was unable to escape the harsh impressions of his childhood which printed the gloomy character of the family on his own mind. This indelible mark was one with which he had to come to terms; it prevented the development of healthy feelings and produced his growing conception of his destiny as one who is different, as the lonely exception. It became his second nature to such an extent that in time he was only really himself when the *mood* of "melancholy" was upon him. But unlike those who are truly depressed, he found this mood a strength rather than a weakness. It became the "passion," the constant preoccupation with his own life-experience of his father's fate, without which he was quite unable to produce. In fact this mood became the indispensable foundation for his thinking and writing. This phenomenon is well-known in many artistic natures who would not for any price be without the changes and fluctuations in their dispositions which serve as background music to their spiritual production. Without it they feel poor and shallow. Schubert, who played with his own musical inspirations so skilfully, once cried: "They talk about gay, happy music. I do not know what gay, happy music is."

The quotations mentioned above speak for themselves. Psychiatrists speak of a *folie à deux,* which is a shared condition psychically forced upon one person by another. Such a psychic imposition is the only connection that can be claimed between the psychic sufferings of Kierkegaard and those of his father. But it is still only a superficial resemblance, something very different from real identity.

To put the matter quite correctly: Søren Kierkegaard's "melancholy" was a complex phenomenon, partly an expression of a fragility of mind not uncommon among the members of a manic-depressive family who have not themselves inherited that predisposition, and partly the result of violent influences from the environment. To the latter belongs what Kierkegaard described as "the most terrible," viz., the father's cruel and self-reproaching confessions about his own erotic life. Finally, the word melancholy is a collective name for Kierkegaard's own peculiar poetical frame of mind, his spirit's own favourite form.

Since the view that Kierkegaard suffered from genuinely morbid (i.e., endogenous) depression still has some advocates, it should be emphasized that the opposite opinion, argued in the present book, is very close to that of P. A. Heiberg,[1] the earliest Danish Kierkegaard scholar, who incidentally had first hand knowledge of the Kierkegaard family. This is perhaps more significant as his investigations were not considered in preparing the present study.

Heiberg argued strongly that Kierkegaard's life should not be seen as a medical case-history but rather as a story of self-recovery, as a life-long struggle to shake off the oppressive and constraining inhibitions produced by the environment he had known from earliest childhood. With many quotations Heiberg shows that Kierkegaard never used the word "melancholy" except in connection with the depressing conditions of his childhood and adolescence. The following is one of his examples: "(I) have from my earliest years been melancholy and reserved, have never felt the joy of childhood, have never experienced what carefree childhood means . . . being an object

---

[1] Heiberg's book was written in 1895. The quotations in the following paragraph are translations of passages from this work.

of anxiety to myself." It was, of course, the father who filled his soul with anxiety, who made him an "object of anxiety" to himself with the severe demands of his own agonizing interpretation of Christianity. Heiberg continues pointing out that Kierkegaard defends himself against the views of his father and that "mentally he was basically and eminently healthy," and that he was not overcome by real (i.e., morbid) melancholy ("Tungsind"). He notes that Kierkegaard compensates for the joys of childhood by developing a *life of imagination* that makes him capable of deceitfully hiding his acquired, instilled melancholy under the cover of a gay, witty, easy-going, and sarcastic appearance. This deceit became his only pleasure and reconciled him to his fate. Heiberg puts the matter very vividly: "There exists a clandestine love affair between his melancholy and his imagination. There is a certain erotic-poetic tone in Kierkegaard's style when he depicts his overwhelming melancholy and its insuperable, enchanting power. It sounds almost like Romeo depicting his first love." Heiberg listened to this siren song that Kierkegaard himself sings about his "deep melancholy" and saw that he was able to transpose it into "a mask of ease, restless life, and exuberant gaiety." But all this required more than mere imagination. In his struggle for liberation Kierkegaard also employed his penetrating dialectic capacity. It was this which enabled him to contemplate his "melancholy" from outside, as an object of thought, not simply as a crippling fact, as those who are really ill know it.

Finally Heiberg, himself a graduate though not a practitioner of medicine, points out that when Kierkegaard uses the word "inheritance" in connection with his own melancholy, he does not distinguish between genuine and false inheritance, between genetic inheritance from the family and the early, acquired deviation of mood impressed upon him by the gloomy temperament of his father. In fact, in Kierkegaard's usage, this work means the externally acquired transference of the morbidity of his father.

This should help us to understand the real nature of Kierkegaard's position. On the one hand he was trapped in a straight-jacket while on the other his healthy instincts drove him to struggle toward his own liberation. But his situation was ambiguous: at one and the same time he must preserve his reverence toward his own unhappy father and also guard his and his family's secrets. This deceit had two grounds: a desire to conceal the transferred melancholy and a desire to conceal the morbid guilt feelings of his father.

It follows from the above that the conclusions of the present book accord very well with those of P. A. Heiberg's penetrating work (1895) based upon his familiarity with the family and the *Efterladte Papirer* [Posthumous Papers].

# 2

# Emotional Life

Imagine to yourself a small, delicate late-comer growing up in a home without laughter, close to an aging father who cast the burden of his soul upon all his surroundings. The father is a man of few words, hiding oppressive secrets that might at any time be revealed in unexpected confessions, as discharges from the storm of a dark mind. Add to this the supervision of a brooding, sensitive, self-reproachful, and intellectually precocious older brother. You will then understand that it was these oppressive and very private surroundings that became decisive for his basic beliefs and, later, for his future life. These are more than enough to explain the exaggerated aesthetic sentiments and reflexively explanatory mood of melancholy that followed Kierkegaard through his life. It is not necessary to introduce any genetic factor as a further explanation and, moreover, there is no evidence of such a factor in either his published writings or in his papers.

In this connection it should be emphasized that Kierkegaard's emotional life was *homogeneous and stable* throughout the whole of his lifetime. The single exception, mentioned below, was that the passion of his mind became stronger with the passing of the years. He did not have the immediate and extroverted emotional level of the true manic-depressive which fluctuates with changes in its surroundings. Nor can this be found in his use of indirect communication in the authorship, in his irony, or in his reserved behaviour which was really a form of retreat conditioned and fostered by his isolation and loneliness. On the contrary, he was being straightforward and the sources of warmth, which in spite of all bubbled in his inner being, were simply finding their way to the surface along peculiar channels.

What is characteristic of Kierkegaard (and this is obvious to everybody) is his extraordinary intellect which was partly inherited and partly acquired in the atmosphere of his home and the emotional life that developed against this background. The *intellectual world* was his kingdom. Here he was as a fish in water, as a dolphin playing upon the waves. Here he was in an element in which he excelled. He was himself aware that he was a man of reflection and that no emotions could come to him without being at once translated into reflection. This was the source of his virtuoso ability to describe feeling at the cost of knowing the immediate feelings themselves. He was only really moved when he wrote on some religious question. Here outbursts of feeling would be transformed into moods of inwardness (*Inderlighed*, a key word), humility, and gratitude. The chapter heads of his books alone are fascinating in their mixture of deep spiritual logic and their surprising insight into the religiously moved mind of a lonely man who is capable of complete openness only before his God. Consider the following from *Edifying Discourses*. "The Edification Implied in the Thought that in Relation to God We Are always in the Wrong," "To acquire One's Soul in Patience," "How can the Burden yet be light, when the Suffering is heavy?," "The Joy in the Thought that it is not the Way which is narrow, but the Narrowness which is the Way," "Love Believes all things—and yet is never Deceived," "Love Hopes all things—and yet is never put to Shame," "The Joy of it—That when I 'gain all' I lose nothing at all," etc. In expressions like these Kierkegaard is unequalled. The mood is that of the religious hymn writer Brorson [2] but the moving part is the insight into spiritual matters, in the afterthoughts, in his spirit's happiness with which, by the mastery of language, he reaches divine depths. The more he thinks and reflects, the richer he becomes. There was always a personal sensitivity, fine as filigree, winding like a vine over the emerging idea, however strong and consistent its logic. All those who admire Kierkegaard as a writer have to admit that this ability to call forth pictures and images by means of thought and language is the most peculiar characteristic of his emotional life. In Kierkegaard this

---

[2] Hans Adolph Brorson (1694-1764) was a distinguished Danish writer of hymns and humble, serene tunes which attracted Kierkegaard throughout his life.

takes place on a very high level, not, as with manic-depressive persons, in the elementary and vital feelings.

But, as already mentioned, Kierkegaard is passionate in spite of all this and especially so during the last seven or eight years of his life. Nevertheless, in 1844 he writes: "Let no one misunderstand all my talk about passion and pathos to mean that I am proclaiming any and every uncircumcised immediacy, all manner of unshaven passion" (*Dru*, 488. *Pap*. V A 44). Even his main thesis that one must grasp the paradox through the passion of faith should, according to him, not be understood passionately but, rather, as a final point in the train of his thought. This however must be seen as self-interpretation. His passion was latently present and it began to come gradually to the surface as more and more doors closed before him and he was left alone in complete isolation.

In *The Point of View* Kierkegaard for once speaks from his heart with surprising immediacy and without irony: "This was an indescribable alleviation to a sense of resentment which smouldered in me from my childhood; because, long before I had seen it with my own eyes, I had been taught that falsehood, pettiness, and injustice rules the world—I often had to think of these words in *Either/Or*: 'If ye but knew what it is ye laugh at'—if ye but knew with whom ye have to do, who this flâneur is!'' (*Point*, pp. 52f.). Kierkegaard here confesses that he has had a passionate feeling of anger throughout his entire adult life and that its origins can be traced back to impressions received in his home as a child. In the last chapter of this book we shall return to this point. For the moment we shall interpret this passage as the reaction of a lonely man who has difficulties in communicating with others. These difficulties were caused by his disposition and environment and, in his first years as a writer, were consciously reinforced and complemented by his behaviour as an idler and playboy, behaviour intended to support and conceal the pseudonymns of the early authorship. This affliction was partly self-induced but Kierkegaard was no misanthrope as was Schopenhauer; on the contrary, he was, at least to a certain extent, ostracized by others. More precisely, his relations with his fellow human beings were ambivalent and ambiguous; in a word, he wanted others and yet was sceptical of them. The reactions of approach and avoidance fought for dominance in his mind and the latter won when he, like Brorson, turned his mind away from the world. The passion that was created by this ambivalence had many roots such as the growing realization that he was and would for ever remain a Kierkegaard, bound by the family's unique dispositions, aims, and lifestyle, "alone with yourself and your God." Added to this was an increasing concentration on the world of his own ideas of the truth of which he himself became more and more convinced and, perhaps, his inherent Jutland obstinacy which, in his understanding, could not tolerate any compromise.

This passion must be regarded as a projection of his ambivalent relationship to his father which bound him at the same time as it demanded his liberation. He was never able to throw off this burden. He might have freed himself when his father died and become himself in a much richer sense without the yoke of the past. But he did not choose this solution that might have cured him of the traumatic experiences of his childhood and given him a place in the intellectual world as a *primus inter pares*. It was, as we shall see, sublime loyalty that prevented him from throwing off the constraints and burden of his father.

The passionate element in Kierkegaard's work developed from personal problems and was neither primarily nor necessarily related to his personality as a writer. His superior, innate intelligence might have developed even more brilliantly and with fewer strains than it did. But the tensions remained and showed themselves throughout the short span of his life in conflicts with other intellectuals, with the church, and lastly with the society as a whole. These conflicts could not be solved and were woven into the literary production and became its strongest driving force. On the other hand, Kierkegaard's feelings toward his father, though only rarely displayed, were always strong and passionate, always forgiving in spite of despair, always thankful in spite of their compulsion. His father was the only person toward whom Søren could express his feelings freely and openly both in life and in death. Not even toward Regine was he able to open himself spontaneously and freely; though he was in love (as much as he was able to be in love), his lips were closed. He had already set out on the lonely voyage of his life with sealed orders.

One cannot get the least bit closer to Kierkegaard by seeing his life in terms of what are surely no more than questionable genetic factors. But one can do so by imagining oneself present in the wool-merchant's home, sensing the atmosphere, and witnessing the mental battles that were fought there, man to man, in the mind of each individual.

Kierkegaard's contemporary, the great Danish artist J. Th. Lundbye also failed in his relationship with women. But the predispositions for defeat were different in the two men. Lundbye was a genuine manic-depressive character and what destroyed his aspirations for happiness was his pathological feeling of *worthlessness* when it came to binding himself with a woman. He studied *Stages on Life's Way* but recognized regretfully that Quidam's solution would not do in his case. He could not be content with woman as an idea but had to have her as a creature of flesh and blood. For the completely reflective Kierkegaard, however, a spontaneous love-affair was an impossibility, a mistake, from the start. He must obey the sealed orders that commanded him to pursue the ideas of his mind and aspire toward the final religious breakthrough along the winding path of suffering and paradox. Toward Regine he practiced "repetition" by marrying her spiritually for eternity. This was not a well calculated escape but rather the only way in which he could be faithful. He was able to lead this double life through his *self-confidence* in his vocation and his spiritual strength enabled him to follow his demon and obey its call, sacrificing his life for the idea. He was under the rule of a stern master who would not tolerate any "Regina" at his side. Lundbye lacked these strong qualities. He was straightforward and human whereas Kierkegaard was under the inhuman demands of the ideal. The apparently common fate of these two in their relationship to women was based upon diametrically opposite predispositions and completely different abnormalities. Lundbye grieved while Kierkegaard worked his way toward his own liberation.

# 3

# The Gift of Language

When outsiders do pathographic analyses on the work of poets and writers they must approach the task with utmost care. Every feature that may be interpreted as a manifestation of illness may, with equal justice, be treated as the result of the poet's unusual personality and gift of language. In other words, in order to make the right decision, one must be as familiar with the forms of expression of genius as with the phenotypes of the mentally ill. Many mistakes are made in this area by taking a one-sided view. Similarly, other mistakes are caused when the outer conditions of the subject's life are not adequately investigated. In fact, when examined closely, many mental phenomena can often be explained in a natural way without having resort to pathographic interpretations.

The latter type of mistake was common among the earlier studies of Kierkegaard's supposed disorder. This is illustrated in the treatment of the famous note from May 19, 1838: "An indescribable joy so mysteriously inflames us as the Apostle's cry issues forth, unprovoked: 'to please you, I repeat, to please you'" (my translation. *Pap.* II A 228). This sudden improvement in feeling has been taken as clear proof of a manic change of mind and thus as a cardinal symptom of Kierkegaard's manic-depressive condition. But besides the fact that such changes of mood are within the range of what is usually considered normal, there is an even more obvious explanation. He had left his home a few months before and settled in Løvstræde to get away from his father. When the latter visited him on May 5, his twenty-fifth birthday, they were reconciled in spite of the shocking revelations concerning his father's life and soon afterward, about May 19, Kierkegaard moved back into his father's house. This indescribable joy is testimony that these two inseparable persons had re-established their old tie. The earthquake, which I would date May 5, opened to Kierkegaard the abysses of his father's tortured mind and stemmed from the father's conditioned disclosures of his childhood sins on the moors, of sexual offences (accompanied by warnings against sexuality) and, finally, speculations in German currency that resulted in large profits for himself and bankruptcy and suicide for his business associate in Hamburg. But in fact all this gave Søren a more sincere understanding of and sympathy for the old man. Consequently, even this ''indescribable joy'' can be explained in purely natural terms.

But let us return to the evaluation of Kierkegaard as a writer. We shall first have to consider Kierkegaard's remarkable powers over language in order to distinguish a talent for writing from what is merely psychotic expression. It was the flowing exuberance of Kierkegaard's mind that dictated his style. Style for its own sake was hardly necessary for him. In those moments, when he forgot the knotty philosophical and theological phrases and let himself go, the wealth of his ideas and his literary imagination enabled him to create passages of a moving musical quality in which the language became his and gave him the images and literary mosaics precisely when he needed them. In such gifted moments he was able to create, by his continued poetical inspirations, a literature such as had never before been seen in Denmark. He himself has told us that, from the moment he began to feel like a writer at twenty-one years of age until his very last hour, his thoughts grew freely and even with an annoying vigour and that at no time did the lyrical muse fail him. In fact, it is not possible to show any fluctuations, upwards or downwards, in his unique poetical ability.

In his crushing article against P. L. Møller in the periodical *Fædrelandet* [*The Fatherland*] on December 27, 1845 Kierkegaard wrote that he is continuously fascinated simply by creativity, that he ''is satisfied with the divine enjoyment of philosophical thought,'' regardless of whether it attracted readers or not. He found ''the joy of eternity in the occupation of thought and the pleasures of eternity satisfied''; he has ''found what will occupy me day after day, even if it should please the Lord to add another twelve hours to the day.'' In

*The Point of View* the same theme is developed more clearly: "Since I became an author I have never for a single day had the experience I hear others complain of, namely, a lack of thoughts or their failure to present themselves. If that were to happen to me, it would rather be an occasion for joy, that finally I had obtained a day that was really free. But many a time I have had the experience of being overwhelmed with riches, and every instant I bethought me with horror of the frightful torture of starving in the midst of abundance—if I do not instantly learn obedience, allow God to help me, and produce in the same fashion, as quietly and placidly as one performs a prescribed task" (*Point*, p. 70). The following quotation could stand as a motto for any divinely gifted writer: "... I would give all, and along with that my life, to be able to find what thought has more blessedness in finding than a lover in finding the beloved—to find the 'expression,' and then to die with this expression on my lips. And, lo! it presents itself—thoughts as enchanting as the fruits in the garden of a fairytale, so rich and warm and heartfelt; expressions so soothing to the urge of gratitude within me, so cooling to my hot longing—it seems to me as if, had I a winged pen, yes, ten of them, I still could not follow fast enough to keep pace with the wealth which presents itself" (ibid., p. 67). And again in another passage: "It is said of the 'poet' that he invokes the muse to supply him with thoughts. This indeed has never been my case, ... but on the contrary I have needed God every day to shield me from too great a wealth of thoughts ... I could sit down and continue to write for a day and a night, and again for a day and a night; for there was wealth sufficient for it. If I had done it, I should have been broken" (ibid., p. 68). He has only one thing to do and that is to control himself by writing in quiet obedience to his Creator. Thus he sits quietly as a schoolchild under supervision and carefully writes his letters, nicely and neatly.

Kierkegaard noted that "minor circumstances," when fully developed by the imagination, could bring him to a depressed state—"... and, lo! there developed from this a mood, and precisely the mood I had use for in relation to the work I was then occupied with, and precisely at the right place" (ibid., p. 72). This is the essence of the true poet's mind with thoughts always ready, always forthcoming. There is nothing disturbed in all this which is but the talent belonging to Kierkegaard's unique nature. It would be more to the point to question the inconstancy of thought of the average person but in Kierkegaard's case one must take account of his genius and give it more weight. Moreover, full as they were, his thoughts centre logically on the content that he wished to express and nowhere can there be found irrelevant, incoherent associations. A central theme governs his writing and gives it depth and consistency.

As already mentioned, Kierkegaard is really in his element when writing simply for the mere pleasure of it; this can be clearly seen in the gay and witty *Prefaces* directed against the poet J. L. Heiberg. Since his style overflows with a multitude of images and metaphors, this has been taken as a manifestation of a disturbed and heightened mental state. But why? This again confuses abnormality with the natural talents of an excessively vigorous writer. Kierkegaard began writing when he was twenty-one with the excellent, witty, and superior essay "Yet Another Defence of Women's Eminent Talents." Since it was published anonymously the public thought that it had been written by Heiberg: who else would be able so to master this light style? But it was in fact the young theological student jumping straight into literature completely equipped from the beginning. This essay is from a period in which, according to the pathographs, Kierkegaard is usually considered "normal in every respect."

But this first little work is obviously written in the same tone as *Prefaces* (from 1845 when he is supposed to be sick) and it is in the same ironical style. To repeat: A literary product that is the result of an abnormally elevated mind is different from the work of a genius in that it is interwoven with irrelevant digressions of a plain and banal content, that it soon becomes confused, that the thread is lost and the presentation ends in a confusing mixture of accidentally emerging ideas.

Kierkegaard's light works are quite different. One consistent idea runs through the whole and is illustrated by a myriad of precise images all of which are to the point. Like a flock of birds they come to his paper, each one bringing a new idea that can be fitted into the work. This is the way of an experienced writer. Kierkegaard had all the necessary prerequisites in abundance: imagination, particularly in respect to language, and a well developed plan of the work to which he adhered strictly without for a moment loosing its guiding thread. His exuberance is not a digression but a consequence of his ability to express in a thousand ways what was on his mind. Similarly, the mood, be it ironical or sincere, is always maintained; it is the constant presence that holds the reader. Only prose that uncompromisingly pursues its central purpose in spite of the suggestive power of its images, is able to do that. Strindberg's prose has the same consistency and logical strength but it is harder and less fertile.

The arguments contained in these few remarks on Kierkegaard's style should have convinced the reader that his literary production shows no signs that he wrote from an unhealthy state of mind and, even less, that he wrote because of such a state. We must free Kierkegaard's reputation as a writer from such mistakes and recognize that it is based upon a more solid and natural foundation, namely, his unique genius. It may be useful to compare his writings with the inconsistency of manic thought that is characteristic of some of Grundtvig's works,[3] in particular those from his later years (*Brage-Snak, Den Christelige Børnelærdom*) which mix the central point with other confusing features as described above. It is a style that is clearly different from that of Kierkegaard. Grundtvig was forced off his course by accidental thoughts whereas Kierkegaard moves steadily ahead in spite of the abundance of his ideas. The result follows naturally: in the latter case the reader is held firmly by the style while in the former the intensity diminishes and the impression is lost in trivial and unimportant whims. Grundtvig, the famous poet, was clearly a manic-depressive.

To Kierkegaard language was always the vehicle of thought. It never ran uncontrolled on its own. It is the mark of the born writer that his pains in creating a lively, personal style never show. His pen runs smoothly along the lines. Between the lines is his style, as a humming of his spirit, a *je ne sais quoi*, thrown into the text with a delicate hand. It is a phenomenon of the music of language in that the basic mood is magically conveyed to the paper in the same way that an Italian continuo for strings, with its gay and delicate tone, is always bright with its own inner logic. This was Kierkegaard's style when it was inspired (as it usually was) and it seems pointless to describe it in medical terms which deprive it of its divine and intangible qualities.

---

[3] N. F. S. Grundtvig (1783-1872) was a famous Danish poet and clergyman and founder of the folk high schools.

# 4

# Dread

Neither in the *Papers* nor in *The Point of View* nor indeed in any other place does Kierkegaard ever mention dread—the most horrifying word in the language—as something that he had personally experienced in the course of his own development. He does however speak of it as having a personal connection in the following passage: "The dread with which my father filled my soul, his own frightful melancholy, and all the things in this connection which I do not even note down. I felt a dread of Christianity and yet felt myself so strongly drawn towards it" (*Dru*, 841. *Pap*. IX A 411). Elsewhere in the *Papers* similar thoughts are recalled: "To construe a child strictly under the qualification 'spirit' is an act of cruelty, in a way is like killing him, and has never been Chrisitanity's intention" (*Hong*, 2, 1215. *Pap*. VIII, 1 A 663).

In quotations of this kind dread is not to be taken in its distinctly psychological sense, as the response to an immediate threat to what is innermost in the personality or to the terrifying possibility of the destruction of the "I." Kierkegaard does not seem to be concerned with the concept of dread as related to such private and personal experiences. From this we may conclude that if Kierkegaard had suffered from severe depressive episodes at all, which I doubt, they were not, at any rate, of an anxious character. In the quotations mentioned, dread should be interpreted as the horror induced by the familiar but external incidents in the family connected with the father's character. The earthquake in May 1838 was such a terror. It related back to his own experience of the erotic and became decisive in his relationship to Regine.

Beause of his reflective nature Kierkegaard rejected the word dread as meaning depression and changed it into a concept, a term with a precise philosophical sense, which is somewhat confusing since dread is ususally considered to be a concrete psychological state. It was from this philosophical angle that he wrote his book *The Concept of Dread*. In this book dread is analyzed as a determination of what he calls spirit; it is a symptom indicating that man both wants and fears to enter this category. Man has the double possibility of living either in the immanent (this world) or in the transcendent (the world of the spirit, the kingdom of freedom) and between these two possibilities is the steadily recurring situation of choice. Here dread appears as an expression of the extreme qualitative difference between the two roads man may choose. According to the *Papers* "... anxiety is (not) an imperfection ... to the contrary, the greatness of anxiety is the very prophet of the miracle of perfection, and inability to become anxious is a sign of one's being either an animal or an angel ..." (*Hong,* 1, 97. *Pap.* V B 53:23). Hence, it is an entirely normal state. And further: "Is the sensual not pure, i.e., penetrated by the moral, appearing as dread's anger? Dread is never present when the sensual becomes the animal ..." (my translation. *Pap.* V B 53:33), here taking animal as an arbitrary abstraction from spirit. Dread is to be found where the "possibility of freedom" is present; it is "subjectivity's *discrimen* (ambiguity)." The individual senses the possibility of passing into the sphere of spirit but reconsiders because he knows that this would mean at the same moment confessing his guilt and sinfulness. Philosophically, dread means doubt, unwillingness or lack of courage to experience existential self-knowledge. Put another way, Kierkegaard wants to show that psychology must admit that in any situation of choice there is, in spite of certain determinations, the free possibility of acting in two very different directions—toward freedom: "the good" or toward inhibition and limitation: "the evil." Every moment the individual stands within and before his own life and what he realizes is always a function of his nature. When he acts and makes a decision he is at the same time participating in the formation of his life; he gives life, in its totality, his own little turn toward good or toward evil. In this he is beyond any simple reflective or one-sided psychology. Spirit becomes one with a concrete way of

life, an ontological determination where all responsibility is personal.
Dread becomes a sign, even on the psychological level, of that step
into the decisive, qualitative situation that both attracts and repels
because of the absolute difference between the two possibilities.

It was the problem of the erotic, and with it, of sexuality, that set
Kierkegaard working on his profound explanations of the concept of
dread. These problems provided him with a personal point of departure. The erotic was to him the most outstanding example of the clash
between the "angel" and the "animal." This conflict was pushed to
extremes by the double relationship that existed within him since his
inclinations toward Regine were aroused at the same time that his
father was giving him sombre warnings against the erotic. The
fatherly idol frightened him away from it as a force that could destroy
a man's life. Kierkegaard spent all his energy convincing himself that
if the erotic were sinful in itself then it may become the *original sin,*
an inheritance that passes from father to son. He wrote (in the
*Papers* from 1844) that he wanted to "trace the effects of original sin
on his own or any other human's consciousness." He might have
added "and on a family," the inherited feature being its tendency to
prefer the animal to the angel. Kierkegaard's attitude toward the
father, to whom the erotic was sinful or the power of the flesh, meant
that he was tied to the father with his sins and that he wanted to suffer
with him. He wanted to take over and carry the sufferings of the father
in his own way by renunciation and asceticism. However this noble
idea was combined in his mind with sexuality now conceived as a kind
of mental demon. He saw how its power might degenerate and how it
had degenerated within the inner circle of his family. This must not
repeat itself; rather, he would take up the cross and endure the
suffering. He did that by sublimating the problem philosophically as a
struggle between flesh and spirit. His father's awful warning turns up
in many guises in the *Papers*. The statement "No man can know with
certainty how many children he has had . . . " is repeated twice in the
diary from 1844.

So for Kierkegaard the concept of dread is not an expression of
personally morbid experiences of dread (paroxysms). Nor is it the
expression of a vulgar transformation of an inhibited sexuality into
fear. Rather, it is the repercussion of the shocking experiences within
his narrow circle of relatives, reflected in a mind that was uncondi-
tionally bound to a family living under that cloud and aware of its own
peculiarities. Consequently, we cannot find the symptom of dread as

a manifestation of pathology in Kierkegaard any more than as a sign of depression in its true sense. For Kierkegaard, "the thorn in the flesh" had nothing to do with dread or sexuality; it was what he *called* melancholy but, as mentioned earlier, it was actually one with his own externally conditioned disposition.

In this connection it should be added that it is false that Kierkegaard never mentioned his mother. In the *Papers* concerning *The Concept of Dread* we find in the margin these notes:

> Thus it is as if I were consecrated to her.
> God—and my deceased mother.
> who is treated unlovingly.
> recklessly to risk one's honour. (1844)

This note must mean: "I must be faithful to myself, never forget Regine, God and the mother who was faithful to her husband, in spite of all."

# 5

# The Leap

Kierkegaard's original doctrine of the leap is an indeterministic theory about the life of the will and the capacity to make a decision. It should be at least briefly mentioned in any account of his psychology as it is both illuminating and symptomatic of the complicated and, to a certain degree, incompatible conditions and considerations to which he had to adjust his mental life. He was enough of a thinker to see the difficulty of combining philosophical thinking with belief in an historical revelation. His problem was to find a formula that would do justice to both thought and faith. Philosophically, it became the doctrine of the leap and the individual's existential relationship to it. Religiously speaking however, this leap meant that the individual simultaneously embraces the paradox of faith. In this way Kierkegaard was able to maintain his inherited faith and at the same time remain a thinker. In his mind the two had to be combined in a way which would not betray either. Consequently the notion of the leap became a strange—some say forced—combination of clear philosophical thinking and a deeply personal commitment to his inherited tradition. It stands as one of the most earnest attempts that has ever been made to combine apparently incompatible opposites. The "free" leap by which all thinking ends became to him a "category of despair" as was also Christianity itself. "... [A]ll Christianity is rooted in the paradoxical, whether one accepts it as a believer, or rejects it precisely because it is paradoxical. ... [I]t lies in fear and trembling,

which are the desperate categories of Christianity, and of the leap"
(*Postscript,* p. 96). "Christianity was also a desperate way out when
it first came into the world, and in all ages remains such; because it is a
desperate way out for everyone who really accepts it" (ibid., p. 96).

The writer of these words was a thinker in despair, one who at
any price had to combine clear thinking with reverence toward the
spiritual legacy of his home. Tradition was victorious over the despair
that became one with the struggle for the eternal in man. The father
watched over Søren's shoulder as he formulated his thoughts on the
leap. At the same time, and in his calmer moments, his certainty about
its reality was grounded in a strong philosophy which he could never
allow himself to reject.

In *The Concept of Dread* Kierkegaard explores the question
from an ethical-religious perspective, as a struggle of the personality.
Here the problem of the ethical-religious decision is presented. As
already mentioned, he holds that there comes a moment when, liter-
ally, the decision is not planned and then carried out as part of a
continual process but rather steps into reality as a new event in the
historical process of the spirit. This leads either to the good or the bad
because the spirit is synonymous with what is really happening,
because it is an ontological determination of being. The leap is that
moment, outside consciousness in the moment of the act of the will,
when one passes from possibility to actuality. Kierkegaard wants to
include not just the impersonal reason but both the central personality
and the spirit as that by which the course of events is carried out in
reality. He does not dismiss the preceding history of the individual as
having no influence in his choice, but he emphasizes that with every
choice one is at the gates of the kingdom of freedom where the finite
touches the eternal. This is a step beyond all psychology, here referred to as approximation, and is the most meaningful and decisive
step in the entire process. In the leap one throws oneself, in spite of
every consideration, into an element that is beyond the personal, like
a swimmer who dives from a diving-board without the security of
knowing precisely where he will fall.

But Kierkegaard also seems to have had a scholarly concern with
the phenomenon of the leap in areas of the mental life other than the
personal. In the *Papers* from 1844 there is an undated passage about
*the leap as a stage in thinking: All analogy and induction can only be
established by a leap*. The word leap is printed in the text not only in
italics but also in heavy type so that it carries a double emphasis. Here

the leap is presented as a discontinuous or intermittent feature which is a fundamental phenomenon in all logical thinking that is not deductive, the latter being for Kierkegaard "essentially identity." Everything that is new is brought forth by inductive thinking and this is as true of scientific investigation and everyday thought processes as it is in the case of personal decisions. There is a certain affinity between this inductive thinking and the mental attitude Pascal calls *esprit de finesse,* that sure discrimination or instinctive feeling for the right. Pascal's other type of mental attitude is directed by the *esprit de géométrie* and obtains its results by an analytic, deductive procedure.

Kierkegaard was absolutely right in asserting the discontinuity of thinking and he did not need to resort to his painful notion of despair and paradox as the only means of escape from his philosophical cross. On empirical and philosophical grounds he might have been content to point out that the larger part of the psychic life takes place in the unconscious, that the stream of thoughts is discontinuous, and that all conclusions and decisions present themselves in the form of minor or major intuitions from the realm of the unconscious. To put it briefly: "In the end, all analogy and induction may only be reached by a leap" not only in the most personal areas but wherever a thought process occurs and new thoughts are created. This is a sound psychological point of view. He is certainly eager to present the ethical man as having a consistent character and able to will repetition. Kierkegaard was himself extemely consistent in his own life style but in his passion he was carried beyond the philosophical point he had introduced and which would have been sufficient to support his teachings on the leap. These teachings are quite sound psychologically and there is no need to justify them by reference to transcendental ideas.

Kierkegaard stood in a close relation to Lessing who introduced the category of the leap[4] in opposition to Hegelianism. Lessing did not himself venture to make the leap but he was sincere enough (and ironical enough) to recognize its necessity if one was to move from "accidental historical truths to necessary and eternal truths of reason." Lessing thought the gap between these two categories much too wide for his old legs and heavy head. Like Kierkegaard he knew that those who leap "must be alone in the task and also alone in understanding rightly that it is an impossibility," the latter applying

---

[4] Kierkegaard discusses Lessing's attitude to "the leap" in *Concluding Unscientific Postscript,* pp. 59-113.

especially to Lessing. For Kierkegaard, the leap was always a conscious act in spite of the implicit gap; that is to say, it was "a category of decision," "an act of isolation in that it recommends to the individual that he decide by believing, by the power of the absurd." One cannot help others take the leap "because essentially every human is taught only by God." Kierkegaard might have said "is taught by the sub-conscious powers of the mind." Lessing was fair to Kierkegaard in recognizing the requirements but he refused to accept them for himself. The two men could have maintained a mutual sympathy by realizing that faith develops sub-consciously and is born in the depths of the mind as a sign of grace when the need for it arises.

The philosophers of continuity attack Kierkegaard's account of the leap or ethical decision. Høffding[5] holds that Kierkegaard actually relegates the decision to the moment before the leap. But his argument fails to make the psychological distinction between reflections before and after the will and the act itself. He is quite right in asserting that reflection plays a part in and contributes to the direction of the leap. But the leap itself is by nature what Kierkegaard describes as a moment of discontinuity beyond the scope of reflection. Psychologically it is characterized in Kierkegaard's mind as an intermediary or gap during which the individual momentarily abandons himself, "lets things slide," even though he has later to confirm the decision as his own. If one becomes familiar with the psychology of decision, one will always find this strange moment when one decides, by a difficult process, to put an end to all further speculation by means of a personal act rather than by simply attempting to draw the consequences of preceding considerations.[6] It is well known that one cannot draw absolutely necessary and, in all respects, predictable conclusions by means of reflection. The phenomenon of the will, though now challenged because it cannot be viewed introspectively, is an example of an unconscious act whose only conscious factor is the experience of the gap in the preceding train of thought.

Connected with this is the fact that every act of will demands a certain amount of daring, a personal effort that is not needed for the completion of a logical line of thought. Though one is not usually

---

[5] Harold Høffding (1843-1932) was a noted Danish philosopher, humanist, and friend of William James.

[6] Modern physicists such as W. Heisenberg assert a complementary relation between antecedent considerations and resolution and present the latter as a cutting-off of the former.

aware of this, it belongs to the very nature and conditions of an actively lived life, no matter how conscientious the preparation for the decision. Even the surest prediction may possibly prove itself wrong. Kierkegaard is absolutely right in distinguishing between (impersonal) approximation and (the personal) leap. He is to be credited for stressing both the engagement of the personality in all aspects of the life of the will and the irrational aspect that is always connected with it.

Kierkegaard was consistent as a thinker and always appealed to the disposition of the personality. But in spite of his consistency as a writer, he himself was not a man of will. He saw all the possibilities and analyzed them in finest detail, but he could not move himself and his life as a thinker has been aptly characterized (by C. Fischer) as a zero-existence. He stood at the crossroads describing the ways one may take while he himself remained there without choosing any of them. It is very likely that his intense preoccupation with the problem of the will is related to an unconscious recognition that he had insurmountable difficulties in this area and that these provided a point of departure for this passionate interest in the psychology of the will. It is generally known that writers often attack features of the character with which they themselves have to fight. Henrik Ibsen was also a poet of consistency but, as we now know, had great difficulty in practicing his teachings in his own life. Kierkegaard's lack of will power is a symptom of the particular sensitivity that comprised such a large part of his temperament and that will be investigated in the following chapter.

# 6

# Social Sensitivity

We can trace through the whole of Kierkegaard's short adulthood one personality trait that is of the greatest importance for a comprehensive psychological evaluation but which has been more or less neglected. Briefly, Kierkegaard suffered to an extreme degree from a particular kind of sensitivity that may best be termed social sensitivity.

We all have to come to terms with the problem of evaluation, that difficult problem of achieving harmony and agreement between the judgment we have of ourselves and that which other people and society have of us. Most people succeed in creating a balance between these two, although it is not always perfect or permanent since the personality is being worn continually by the stream of time and events. But for certain natures, finding this balance is a serious problem. Those who are forced by various circumstances into loneliness and isolation must create, on their own and without any healthy corrections from the outside, their own images of themselves as social beings. This easily leads to faulty self-conceptions in the form of under- and over-evaluations of the self, together with solitary sensitivity, vulnerability and suspicion regarding the way in which others judge one's character. These difficulties become even greater if this alienation is rooted in deep personality disturbances that result in painful feelings, conscious or repressed, of inability to fit into the community and find one's place among others. When, besides this feeling of insufficiency, a person is convinced of his superiority and has a strong self-conceit that tells him that he could have become famous had he not been so severely restrained by his fated inhibitions and feelings of inferiority and had he not been forced to the defensive in spite of his desire to join the life of the community—then we have present all the necessary conditions for a severe inner tension and collision. The situation is very ambivalent; the person is pulled in opposite directions and this causes the painful condition of tension. He is grounded in his own solitude and yet, in spite of this, keeps an extremely careful watch for every indication of how his environment perceives and regards him.

Kierkegaard's case was precisely of this type. Though he struggled to realize himself as a member of society, he could not unite his assets and liabilities into an attitude that would enable him to achieve this goal. They would not combine into a single whole in a way which would let him become a member of the party.

His liabilities were many and great. By nature, he was overly sensitive to all influences and judgements and every impression inscribed itself deeply and painfully upon him. His strange, abnormal and isolating upbringing reinforced these features. The extremely radical influence of his father—and the subordinate position of his mother—became for Søren a source of terrible pressure that forced him into a definitive sense of loyalty towards his home. Never would he be able to abandon that special Kierkegaardian nature. From his youth the idea was fixed in his mind that, like the rest of the family, he was an exception, an outsider whose private secrets could not be shared with anyone. With this came a growing recognition of his extraordinary abilities which should have made Kierkegaard confident but which he actually interpreted as a sign that he had a special mission, even a religious duty, to atone for the family's sins. Severe tensions were produced when these inhibiting factors were combined with his desire, unknown to his father, to escape his artificially isolated life. Already at an early age he harboured a suppressed envy of all those who belonged to the community and, in particular, those who by their ability and stature held high positions and towards whom he felt himself equal or even superior. But still he was unable to leave the shelter of family tradition. The opposition seemed strong and even invincible. There he stood with his brilliant assets—his eminent talent for reflection, his connection with contemporary literary circles in Copenhagen, his brilliant play with words, the irony that he used so masterfully, his art of creating moods, the religious inwardness that he transformed into a hitherto unknown verbal art that disarmed even those who were otherwise offended by his sarcasm. But in spite of all this he was still unable to create any immediate contact with the rich and fruitful cultural life that surrounded him. Hence there was no other means of escape than to change his haunted enclosure into a fairy palace where he could freely entertain his ever ready ideas and from which he could still view the world as from a prison window. His imagination transformed his prisoner's cell into a magic castle that, in time, he would not exchange for anything. Making a virtue of necessity, he made isolation uniquely desirable, "the individual" the highest ideal, and "the numerical," the masses, or the "ballotting" crowd contemptible and ridiculous. The problem was never resolved; the tensions between solitude and community continued as an inner struggle throught his life and it grew, as we shall see, year by year until it finally blew up in an explosion. This final result shows to what extent his father had distorted his development and had denied his human needs; it was these which finally forced their way to the surface with the wild strength and overwhelmingly destructive power of a dammed river.

But all this came gradually and we must proceed chronologically. From the start, Kierkegaard chose to keep himself at a distance and to avoid direct communication. In his early youth, from the age of twenty-one to twenty-eight, irony was his favourite means of escape. His first anonymous newspaper articles played on gay irony; in these the young writer enjoyed himself thoroughly and reared his sharpness as one breeds a noble horse. Kierkegaard did not really have very much to say in these articles; his purpose was to expose, in a very sophisticated and skilful manner, his opponent's failing logic. This was gay and subtle fun and was equal to anything in the periodical *Corsair*. Thus from the start Kierkegaard chose the indirect method of simulation as a means of avoiding direct confrontation with his surroundings.

While with the young girls at the Rørdam manse he tried to suppress his "demon's wit" but obviously had difficulty as some unhappy notes in the diary indicate. Free and natural contacts were impossible for him and, in spite of his heroic attempts toward Regine, he backed out at a decisive moment because of his mental peculiarities that required him to use disguise and a code language in order to hide his most innermost secrets.

The aesthetic period of Kierkegaard's authorship soon followed and lasted from 1843 to 1846. In *The Point of View*, written in 1848, Kierkegaard gives a very strange explanation of his behaviour during that period. In fact, he had isolated himself from the public by his carefully staged behaviour and presented himself outside his home as a playboy or idler drifting in the streets and frequenting the theatre. He said that his purpose was "to support the pseudonyms" although it would seem that he had distanced himself sufficiently from them and had clearly let the public know that he was not identical with "Frater Taciturnus" or any of his other Latin authors. Moreover his use of this ironical mask should underline the fact that, although essentially a religious author, he was here appearing parenthetically as an aesthetic one lacking "earnestness." He had to operate in a light genre because essentially he was not the character he made himself out to be in the aesthetic writings. Nevertheless in the same breath he underlines the fact that these writings were indirectly a part of his service to "truth, the idea" and, as such, should certainly be taken quite seriously. Finally, this diversionary tactic helped him to avoid becoming an object of public attention and admiration which would serve only to divert attention from the contents of the works. In fact, he wanted to secure himself against the general tendency of the public to flatter a writer and to shower praise on him instead of heeding his message.

All of Kierkegaard's sophistic machinations seem to have been constructed as bad excuses and they seem to suggest that behind their production lay some private theme that must not be revealed; namely, his aversion to making any move toward community life. However, like his irony in the preceding period, the subtle designs of his behaviour reveal that he did not intend to burn all his bridges; on the contrary, he wanted to maintain "a dialectical connection" with his surroundings. Here again his ambivalence is apparent in that more than ever he is watching for any sign, however small, that might show that he is not appreciated on his merits.

In the following *Corsair* period, Kierkegaard could have changed the direction of his life but did not do so. One might expect that since he now openly presented himself solely as a religious author, he would accept himself and, given his somewhat spurious excuses for his behaviour during the preceding aesthetic period, would present himself openly as the person he was. Clearly he had no more need to be ironical. But it was not to be so; Kierkegaard found a new excuse and means for maintaining his isolation. The *Corsair* itself had a wide circulation among the public, which it both maltreated and educated ironically, and what was the ironist Kierkegaard to do with this rival and competitor? It was obvious that he was not himself above the use of irony. The *Corsair* and its readers regarded him as obstinate. He found a way of escape in a new form of self-torture by demanding to be attacked in the *Corsair* and thus become the victim of the town's laughter and mockery. Thus, he was once again able to develop in the only way that was acceptable to him—in the duplicity of loneliness and watchfulness, both symbolized by his shuttered window. He discovered that "the religious author is always polemical"; he opposed the religious degeneracy reflected in "the nonsense and laughter of this small country," and he stressed his category of the individual even as he conceived himself as an individual standing against the entire mass. "The circumstances are once again right for an indirect communication." For "the religious communication (must not become) too direct or provide me with readers too directly. The reader can (follow my method) and hold himself aloof from any direct relations with myself. For in the place of the aesthetic incognito I now had to face the menace of hoots and laughter which discourages the majority." The "polemical reckoning" must exist in order that "every praise be viewed as an attack and every attack be viewed as insignificant."

It is clear that Kierkegaard rationalized his isolation and that, for deep and well-concealed reasons, wished to maintain his ambivalent position. Indeed it was the only one in which he could thrive. It combined isolation on one hand and an alert combat position on the other and was his only form of contact with those about him. He fluctuated between being pleased and being tortured by his loneliness and deep need to cultivate his inwardness. To an increasing degree he allowed himself to be influenced by the smallest sign that he was misunderstood, criticized, or treated as a special case. At the same time he consolidated much of his personality under the image of himself as an "exception" with a special mission. His inflated and hypersensitive watchfulness for anything relating to the evaluation of his person was always with him and it had a great effect on his moods and on the writings in his diary. Even kind remarks were more and more interpreted as hidden assaults and gradually the sinister glare of a persecution-complex appears in his thoughts.

It is well-known that in Kierkegaard's life a great disproportion gradually developed between insignificant incidents and extended violent reactions. All these matters, which he developed in an imaginary inner drama, came to their fullest expression against the leading cultural personalities of the day. Some of the best known cases will be examined in more detail.

### J. L. Heiberg

In his earliest period as a writer, when he published his witty, anonymous articles in Heiberg's periodical the *Copenhagen Flying Post*, Kierkegaard felt himself under the protection of this influential writer. He was clearly patronized by him, but he felt it as an honour and seemed very comfortable with this arrangement. His sensitivity was shaken for the first time by Heiberg's rather offhandedly written review of *Either/Or* in *Intelligensblade* [*Intellectual Papers*] only ten days after this enormous book of 850 pages was first published. His reaction is recorded in the reply he printed only four days later in *Fædrelandet* [*The Fatherland*] under the ambiguous heading "Thanks to Professor Heiberg." In this reply he tried to help both himself and Heiberg by a resolute twisting of the wording of the review so that its attack is directed against the anonymous reader whom Kierkegaard treats as the real critic. It was not Heiberg, but "the reader" who had failed to concentrate on the work thoroughly and conscientiously. The professor was quite right in thinking that, as he writes, "the reader" should start by leafing through this large work in order to gain a preliminary impression. It is not something which "the reader" can evaluate in a moment. Obviously Kierkegaard wanted to remain on good terms with his feared critic and he approaches him with servile and bowing phrases, keeping his disappointment and his ready satire to himself.

The diary, on the other hand, shows the true nature of Kierkegaard's irreverent attitude toward the mighty. "So today it is a new hymn book that the times require; Heiberg thinks that it is astronomy—perhaps astronomical psalms ought to be selected for the supplement" (*Hong,* 4, 4106). "If Professor Heiberg did not formulate the System, then Professor Rasmus Neilsen did. Let us, however learn to appreciate our benefactors—those good people who are kind enought to help us with their promises." "In his system of logic, Professor Heiberg was all ready to go but the System ended at section 23." And there are others similar to these and written in the same style.

It bothered Kierkegaard that Heiberg had treated *Either/Or* in such a slighting and journalistic manner and he broods over this matter in his typically ambivalent way, at one time admiring and at another mocking. This juxtaposition of minimal cause and lasting mental repercussions came to be typical of Kierkegaard and found its first true manifestation in this connection. In 1844 Heiberg wrote a paper for *Urania* on the great importance of the astronomical year for ethics and aesthetics; a paper in which were interwoven some critical comments on *Repetition*. Kierkegaard reacted publicly with a brilliant little work of genius entitled *Forord* [*Prefaces*, untranslated] that is one long and popular satire on Heiberg as a guide for the people and as a philosopher and writer. Heiberg had promised "to realize within thirty years his plan to publish a system of logic (à la Hegel) as soon as possible to redeem himself since ten years earlier he had promised an aesthetic system and still earlier an ethical and dogmatic system and, finally, *the* System."

Kierkegaard felt vastly superior to Heiberg, both as a writer and as a philosopher and the diary is full of pointed allusions to this self-appointed judge of taste and literature. Unlike Heiberg, he did not want to be "cast as the buffoon in clown literature of the New Year"; he mocked "his poetic copybook writing" and insisted that it must not be confused with style. All such works can be readily recognized "as fringes on Professor Heiberg's *Intellectual Papers*." But, he continues from his heart: "However, where there is talk about ideas, thoughts, about wild passions, about the soul's heartfelt emotions, about despair's cry and the heart's deep sign," yes, here it is all in vain. But he adds with sudden uncertainty: "I wonder what Professor Heiberg will say about this book (*Forord*); rather, I hope people get to know who 'the reader' means." Heiberg's little work had made a deep impression on Kierkegaard's sensitive mind and it was still gnawing there years after he had read it. No one can doubt that Kierkegaard showed an incredible sensitivity in connection with this episode, a sensitivity which became even more apparent in the affair of the *Corsair* and later. Further, his positive-negative attitude or ambivalence toward Heiberg in this matter is manifest and evident.

Heiberg was almost pathetically tolerant in spite of the sharp attacks upon his most sincere efforts. After Kierkegaard's death, he referred loyally in *Københavnsposten* (*The Copenhagen Post*) of 1856 to Kierkegaard's unpublished essay on the performance by his famous wife Johanne Louise Heiberg in *Romeo and Juliet* and recommended it because of "the contempt with which it dismissed the current incompetent dramatic criticism in all its aesthetical thinness and moral wickedness."

### P. L. Møller and Goldschmidt

In the beginning the *Corsair* bestowed only praise and admiration upon this new literary phenomenon, disguised as he was under a number of pseudonyms. But Kierkegaard soon found that there was something slightly wrong in this treatment and he certainly did not want to be regarded as a supporter of the *Corsair*. He therefore provoked a change in the situation. It became a boomerang that bored into his sensitive heart and reinforced his feeling of standing alone for the truth—mocked, ridiculed and rejected. Theoretically he still held the view that the martyrdom of loneliness was his real calling and that a true Christian could have only enemies, but at the same time he was tortured by the fire that he himself had lighted. He suffered from a lack of appreciation and by being made to seem ridiculous and thus his hostile feelings toward his surroundings increased. It is difficult not to label Kierkegaard's attitude in this case masochistic. He seemed consciously to seek out a position where the arrows would be directed against his own breast and he took care in each case to perpetuate the vicious circle.

The starting point was known to be the critic P. L. Møller's article printed in *Gaea* in December 1845.[7] It was a calm and reasonable appraisal that included much praise and admiration but also some criticism that touched Kierkegaard—as usual—at an overly sensitive point. In fact, it referred *to the quality that Kierkegaard had himself* recognized several years before in his diaries as open to criticism. P. L. Møller wrote: "A soul that is lost in reflection. . . . Such a dialectic I have heard used by very hypochrondriacal persons who are ruled by a fixed idea. . . . Nothing is fresh and straightforward, he has to reflect on everything. . . . Despite his intelligence, reflection has become in him a terrible illness." Someone who knows within himself that he suffers from a weakness cannot tolerate its discovery by another. A feeling of inferiority is incited when it, like Evil itself, is even mentioned by name. Kierkegaard was immediately on the attack. He asks to be dressed down, not immortalized, in the *Corsair* and throws

---

[7] The article in question appears on pp. 144-87 of this issue.

contemptuous, angry invectives at this thing which he considers to be the real instigator. In his excellent book *Fra Fyrrerne* [*From the Forties*], Otto Borchsenius characterizes Kierkegaard's personality as one in which "the greatest and the meanest qualities seem to have been strangely mixed, one whose extreme sensitivity might tempt a young satirist (namely, Goldschmidt, the editor of the *Corsair*) to try on Kierkegaard himself 'that ridiculous composition' Kierkegaard had previously found lacking in the *Corsair*" and that he had invited Goldschmidt to supply, "though the result was not entirely to his satisfaction." It all ended with Kierkegaard standing alone on what he himself called "his higher justice," while his contemporaries dismissed him as an eccentric, a strange personality reduced to recording in his diaries, *ad absurdum*, whatever happened. The satiric method of the *Corsair* was, in this case, unusually rude and impertinent and in the midst of it all Goldschmidt decided to resign the office of editor. He felt that he had been party to an attack upon a defenseless man and, further, one who had "that great, wild look . . . and so manifested that 'higher justice' to which Kierkegaard appealed." These circumstances were to Kierkegaard's advantage but they did not give him any mental relief. The damage was already done. He withdrew completely into himself by means of his "polemical instrument." "For the world is not so good that the religious can be assumed to have won or to be in the majority. The essentially religious author is actively polemical; he suffers on account of that or on account of his opposition to what must be considered the specific evil of his time. When it is kings or emperors, popes and bishops and their power which is the evil, then such an author is recognizable by the fact that he is the object of their attack and persecution."

Here Kierkegaard begins to approach that feeling that would later find such violent expression, namely, that the whole world was against him and that he could count only upon his God. It was a great tension that for years held him suspended between the peculiar Kierkegaard tradition with its secrets and solid convictions, and the superior and condescending attitude of the outside world which he found so thoroughly hostile. Further, in the attack by the *Corsair* this hostility was aimed directly at his person which seemed thereby to be placed under suspicion. This tension had finally to vent itself. This happened in what has generally been called "the Church struggle" but which can be better understood as Kierkegaard's unrestrained but nevertheless understandable reaction to his own inner conflicts. His social sensitivity could no longer tolerate the insufferable tension; it had to find release in an explosion. In our description of this explosion, we shall mention another cultural figure with whom Kierkegaard stood in an ambivalent relationship, namely, Bishop J. P. Mynster.

# 7

# Toward the Breaking Point

If one wishes to understand Kierkegaard's psychology it is absolutely necessary to discover an explanation for his last impassioned performance. It is not at all sufficient to refer to the "Church struggle" as simply a battle against the existing Church structure, which in any event he had been waging privately within himself for several years. The real truth is that this chosen spirit spent the last years of his life flinging one anathema after the other at official Christianity, the authorities, and society. In these attacks he employed his linguistic genius in a variety of ways but always he deals with the same monotonous subject. In all he produced nine instalments of "The Instant," sixty-four papers and twenty-two newspaper articles in the period from December 1854 to June 1855; of these, eighty-eight were almost identical in purpose. The attacks were passionate and some almost frenetic. This whole phase had the character of a crisis and in it Kierkegaard never reached his usual sublime level. This period has impressed certain readers because of its swift, polemical attacks but, compared to the production of the preceding years, it is a sad and embarrassing affair. There was only one string left on this unique instrument and on it Kierkegaard played a monotonous but violent tune.

## J. P. Mynster

It was the personality of J. P. Mynster that set this attack in motion and we must begin by explaining Kierkegaard's relationship to him.

Mynster was one of the most difficult public personalities with whom Kierkegaard had to come to terms. He had been his father's priest which was itself an almost insuperable obstacle to any discussion. Further, his Christianity was basically not that far from Kierkegaard's. He was pious, almost "tending toward inwardness"; he spoke and wrote in the spirit of Christianity, was an opponent of Grundtvig, and had reviewed Kierkegaard's *Edifying Discourses* favourably and with understanding (under the signature Kts, from the middle letters of each of his three names). In his work *For Self-Examination* (1851) Kierkegaard even says of Mynster's "sermons" that they "have wanted to effect . . . the same thing that I want, only (I) with a stronger emphasis . . ." (*Self-Examination*, p. 45). The stumbling-block was that Mynster preached "with authority," claiming to be a Christian in the strictest sense whereas Kierkegaard emphasized that as a true seeker after Christ he personally was without authority and that he sought inwardness without "being emptily puffed up to the point of giving (myself) out to be a witness for the truth and encouraging others to wish rashly to be the same, I am an unauthoritative poet who moves people by means of the ideals" (ibid., p.46). Mynster was unsympathetic to this writing and during a visit to the prelate Kierkegaard felt Mynster's condescension as he remarked briefly that this writing "was surely directed against him," the head of the Church into whose hands the true teaching had been put. Once again Kierkegaard was attacked on his "higher justice," his sensibility offended, and his "extreme touchiness" aggravated. The road to a quiet agreement was blocked from both sides by their different emphases. It became painfully annoying to Kierkegaard that this man, this calm and respectable bishop, so well placed in society and in the educated circles, should thus be able to sweep him and his demand for the ideal aside and that he should not even be able to make himself heard. This disproportion became intolerable. He came to have only contempt for this official who planned Christian truths by means of papers and resolutions, who was in his own way a colossus in society but also, and at the same time, a small man when seen from the heights of the ideal. Their relation underscored the gap between his own social poverty and spiritual wealth. And yet, with the respect he had learned and the insufficiency he felt, he admired this "most reverend old man" at the same time as he silently mocked this official "witness to the truth," the latter being his own symbolic and highly combustible little phrase. His higher right should and would sooner or later have the last word even if it should take a revolution. His ambivalence was to become intensified and his tension brought to its extreme limit.

Feelings of reconciliation became more and more alien to Kierkegaard and to make any concessions appeared to be cowardice. Even the most peaceful, indeed benevolent, figures in the culture were not spared in his diaries; it had become a monomania with him to criticize them in a mocking tone. "Professor Sibbern the philosopher now and then has a disturbing influence when he really achieves some little thing." Rasmus Nielsen, his literary executor, was one of "the good persons who are so kind as to help us with their promises." There are similar references to Grundtvig, who was dismissed as simply "stupid," and to Martensen, Rudelbach and Poul Møller, the last of whom was given a beautiful epitaph in the dedication to *The Concept of Dread* before Kierkegaard became so consciously aware of his own inadequacies. He really only admired the deceased, partly because they were not dangerous and partly because he could associate with them in the poetic fantasy of his recollection and refer to them in religious terms. He discouraged all possible friendships and stood alone at last, angular and uncompromising. As compensation he made friends with the common people in the town in the same way as King Christian II who was suspicious of the nobility and joined the common citizens in order to maintain his popularity in other circles. More and more he avoided contact with the cultural life that surrounded him until his isolation became complete. Yet in spite of this he had won the respect and admiration of many groups and had acquired all the qualifications necessary to join the Heiberg or other such groups. He justified his attitude by emphasizing yet more strongly his central category of the individual. This category was the result not only of philosophical and religious considerations but equally of his personal problems, and, especially, of his depressing and increasingly clear realization that all his grave inner difficulties made him quite unfit for open and fruitful contact with others. He could not find a method of contact that suited him and could be adjusted to his special case. The house of Kierkegaard had forbidden him to mingle in high places.

The attack that Kierkegaard eventually launched with such violent fanaticism appeared to be a kind of attack upon the Church. But the desperate radicalism of the charges and his demands for a complete revision of the existing ways of thinking must already suggest that deeply personal matters and passions were concealed behind his theological thoughts. Not enough attention has been paid to the real content and basis of the Church struggle; in fact, it was a cumulative and decisive outburst caused by all the tension which Kierkegaard had collected through the years and which he could no longer control. He had to have a release for all of them, a release that was unconditional and uninhibited. In this violent eruption all his problems were displayed quite openly. It was the surrender of an unhappy and highly gifted man to the tragic complications of his own life. We shall discuss these problems one by one.

1. The basic problem underlying all the others was his attachment to his father and to his family. This attachment was a vice which held him firmly and which, from 1838 until his death, prevented him from working and interacting with the cultural life around him. His desire for liberation lacerated him internally but his bonds were too strong. These remained as a force that was gradually rationalized into two categories, that of the exception ("in the true Kierkegaardian way, alone with God"), and that of the individual in an offensive position vigilant against all outside influences. He maintained both categories consistently and without compromise, with a rigidly unrelenting outlook which was rooted in his loneliness and which had reverence toward the family as its constant mood. In spite of all, Kierkegaard had *his* "system" as Hegel and others had theirs, but in his case it was determined by the circumstances of his upbringing. The so-called Church struggle was his last demonstration that they could not be broken, as is evident from the uncontrolled passion expressed in his reactions.

2. An extreme social sensitivity, a feeling of not being really able to belong to society, was part of Kierkegaard's personality from his earliest childhood and it was coloured by the feeling he *called* melancholy which was not so much gloom as the fated response of an impressionable mind to a sombre family situation. This sensitivity underlay his perpetual struggle with his own desire to meet other people but the latter was destined to fail with the consequence that this craving was converted into opposition and hostility toward the environment for which he secretly longed. This feature is also extremely characteristic of the Church struggle.

3. He also suffered inner conflict at the religious level between the absolute position represented by his father's admonition "to learn to love Jesus properly" and his own confessed position as a "seeker

after Christ," without religious authority. In the *Papers* from 1844 he writes: "I am not a truly religious individual either but rather one constructed with that possibility.... My very great philosophical doubt.... It is dreadful to be able to comprehend the religious need that is so deep and yet to have such a doubt." He also refers to a quotation from the chapter on melancholy from 1847 concerning the possibility of getting closer to himself by thinking his melancholy through together with God on the spot. The whole production at this time was intended to ascertain the distance between his life and what it was to be a Christian in the strictest sense, to determine whether he might call himself a witness to the truth, which in fact he never dared to do. Here again his reverence towards the absolute demands of his father was broken by his thoughtful questioning, his acknowledgement of this quite inconvertible demand and his respect for it. An open struggle against the institutional Church implied equally an open admission that he had not succeeded in following his father's footsteps and accomplishing what was expected from a Kierkegaard. The Church struggle had therefore to become an internal fight against himself in this essential area also; it was a manifestation of his own agony but one which the people of the Church had to confess and suffer as well.

4. As a public character in the intellectual life of his time Kierkegaard suffered from his lack of clarity about how to use his unusual abilities. Was he a poet, a philosopher, or a religious author? He maintained a constant dialogue with himself on this question and he was never able to resolve it and so remained a great question mark to himself at least in this respect. This made it difficult for him to form a personality that he could present in public without creating misunderstanding and confusion. His bond to the family directed him toward self-realization as a religious author but his unique gifts, not fully understood even by those closest to him, directed him toward philosophy and poetry. The celebrated acuity of his mind and his uncommon mastery of the language were innate for Kierkegaard and could not be suppressed. They were part of his nature and were supported by that vague but productive *mood* of melancholy into which he had been forced as a child. Here was yet another weakness, a division that might become an external obstacle to his self-realization. Another factor was that the richness of his thought and his mastery of language combined to raise his religious production to the level of the sublime.

All these private difficulties were his real motivations in the Church struggle which was only indirectly an attack upon the existing Church. It became a symbol of his personal dilemma in all these areas that he could no longer control. It was a postponed clash with his father and the inhuman way in which he had raised Søren, a clash which he had suppressed for sixteen years. There is a straight line from his experiences in childhood (and their reflection in his subsequently acquired disposition) to the uncontrolled outbursts of this final phase.

# 8

# Open Conflict

There are features other than those we have just mentioned that indicate that the Church struggle was an outer form through which Kierkegaard's personal conflicts and difficulties with the community found an outlet. Even the passionate and persistent energy there displayed so suddenly was itself usually precipitated by some minor incident. His reaction to the single phrase "witness to the truth" is a good example of this and stands in sharp contrast to the violent emotion that it provoked. To Kierkegaard this phrase was indeed important. In his book *For Self-Examination* (1851) he had analyzed this phrase and stressed that neither he nor Mynster could in any way lay claim to this title. For his own sake, he would not be "emptily puffed up to the point of giving (myself) out to be a witness for the truth" (ibid., p. 46). "So far as that I have never ventured out, that is not my affair. And whenever anyone in our time might seem to want to venture so far out, I was not disinclined to enter into a polemic against him..." (ibid., p. 46). Here he was thinking of Mynster. Neither he nor Mynster were "enough of a Christian to dare join those who make such an (absolute) requirement" (ibid., p. 45) or to be a witness to the truth in the real sense. Least of all should Mynster be regarded as a witness to the truth; indeed, Kierkegaard believed that he himself deserved that predicate more than this much admired prelate. He was greatly hurt that later at Mynster's funeral service Martensen called him an extraordinary hero of the faith. But in spite of all these understandable circumstances Kierkegaard's attack upon the Church was so fierce and so strongly marked with his personal feelings that these must be seen as the real driving force behind it. If one was to find a real "witness to the truth" he must go at least as far as Nytorv.

His personal discomfort is obvious from the fact that he hesitated for almost a year (from January to December 1854) before reacting to Martensen's funeral oration for his predecessor Mynster. He brooded for this long over how he should treat this matter. He could bear it no longer—but how was he to speak? He felt the sermon as a personal affront to his own most serious endeavours despite the fact that it is most unlikely that Martensen had even thought of Kierkegaard (though he may have done so had he remembered *For Self-Examination*). He seems to have seen the dispute as centring around his own private person and to have forgotten Mynster entirely. His sensitivity was heightened to an extreme degree and he was unable to count the number of insults which he felt were cast at him. His personal views were exposed everywhere. The papers mocked him with the name "Søren," as did Martensen in one article to which Kierkegaard replied with his piece "It is true that my name is Søren." In his anger he resorted to means which were not worthy of him. More and more he withdrew from reality and placed himself in an aggressive and even offensive posture toward everyone and everything. He was no longer attacking Christianity as it appeared around him but, with a nihilistic monomania, was instead a dedicated enemy of society, attacking all its institutions without exception—the press, politics, matrimony, the authorities, the Church as a power in society, and even society as a whole. And all this because of Martensen's use of a simple phrase "witness to the truth." It is clear that it would be quite wrong to explain his attitude with the formula "a genius in a market town," as Georg Brandes[8] attempted to do. One would have to be completely blinded by Kierkegaard's genius not to recognize the tragic and terrible aspect of his behaviour, namely, the morbid disproportion between the cause and the reaction. He retained both the keenness of his mind and his outstanding literary ability but his nuances, his quality and his basic sincerity gave way before an agressiveness that was alien to Kierkegaard and a self-esteem and overes-

---

[8] Georg M. C. Brandes (1842-1927) was a famous Danish critic and European literary figure.

timation of the self that was inconsistent with the character he had exhibited until now. He is "As not many are, perhaps as no other in this land is, justified in having a word to say about what Christianity is" (*Attack,* p. 259). He was a mentally tense, strained man who unloaded his secrets in abnormal outbursts. As we have mentioned already, Kierkegaard had never suffered from self-depreciation as truly depressive natures do; in fact, he suffered rather from a slight self-conceit that was neither abnormal nor unfathomable. But this self-conceit had, by this time, become quite exaggerated and even pathological. He was the only one who was right and all the others were wrong.

There is, in Kierkegaard's last dramatic phase of development, a resemblance (though *not* identity) to the psychological mechanisms that are characteristic of certain paranoid conditions which are also a form of morbid animosity toward society. It can be said that the form of Kierkegaard's behaviour and that of the cantankerous person are the same and that they go a long way to illustrate each other. Roughly a cantankerous development is based upon two conditions—a socially vulnerable disposition which has difficulty finding a position in society, and a concrete event that has hurt the person deeply because he believes himself to be the victim of an injustice, an offense, or a slight—this often with some justification but sometimes without. The person cannot work off the crippling incident and his active temper does not allow him to take the path of resignation. On the contrary, he develops an expanding obstinacy which no one will accept and more and more feels himself mocked and overlooked. This gradually leads him into a lonely battle for his "blessed right" which he wages to the bitter end and in which he feels that the whole "rotten society" is against him. More and more it becomes a battle for its own sake and the ties with the starting point are scarcely any longer visible. But the ambiguity or ambivalence remains in spite of all the activity. Deep in his mind the querulous paranoiac feels his own part in the unhappy development—his vulnerability—but he rejects it all the more strongly in order to insist upon his rights. It is like a snowball that is rolled bigger and bigger and harder and harder, so that it cannot melt away.

Kierkegaard also had an extremely sensitive mind. And he was right, in fact completely right, that Christendom is not identical with Christianity (an old idea that was not invented by Kierkegaard). But no one wanted to listen to him, and his self-chosen isolation precluded the possibility of debating the matter and openly presenting different points of view. He regarded his own views more highly than those of others, and increasingly he encountered coldness, misunderstanding, negligence, condescension, silent resistance and disregard for himself and his claims for the ideal.

His vulnerability increased and he sensed threats against him; minor causes were magnified in ill-concealed criticism of his views and his person. Everyone was against him. He must be sacrificed and allow himself to become a victim. Martyrdom was his means of escape in a society that was so solidly against him. And yet in the middle of this development he maintained two things—his self-assurance, which never left him, and his now unattainable longing for community, a distant dream from the time of his youth.

Another thing that he kept and clung to as a last refuge was his relationship to God. It suppported him in his self assurance and it gave him a spiritual community that more than made up for what he lacked with his fellow men. It is touching to read the publication of the sermon "God's Unchangeableness" issued between numbers 7 and 8 of *The Instant* in August 1855. It expresses sublime calm in the midst of the storm and must have impressed the reading public that was annoyed and angered by the unbridled, sarcastic leaflets that he had published. The sermon had been delivered in the Citadel Church in 1851 and its preface is dated May 5, his forty-first birthday. The possibility of a quarrelsome response was present but he had a firm anchor in his innermost self that protected him from capsizing.

In order not to be misunderstood we repeat: there is a similarity to morbid, cantankerous behaviour but there is no identity. Nevertheless the two forms of response illustrate each other. In the Appendix to this volume (pp. 66-68) one can find a remark that brings the picture into balance.

# 9

# A Portrait

This investigation of Kierkegaard's psychology has been carried far enough to enable us now to present a summary result. The task here, as in all psychiatric research, is to discover how far one can go with reasoning based on normal psychology to explain mental phenomena as manifestations of understandable conditions; only when this fails can one resort to a diagnosis of pathology. The opposite procedure—to establish a pathological diagnosis on the basis of certain phenomenological details and to present all the phenomena of a lifetime in this pathological framework—is unacceptable. An equally important methodological rule is to order the identifiable mental features and events in such a way as to give priority to those that contribute most to the illumination and explanation of Kierkegaard's personality, life-pattern and work and those things that are most deeply and intimately connected thereto. It is rarely of any interest to expose pathological mechanisms having no real connection to the concrete life of the individual. What is valid, on the contrary, is to show how possibly abnormal manifestations could affect mental processes more or less radically—if indeed one is forced to consider such manifestations at all.

In Kierkegaard's case it is beyond doubt that the following factors had a quite decisive influence on his mental development. They may be called Kierkegaard's basic problems and so should receive the highest priority in any description of his condition.

1. His bonds, from earliest childhood, to his family and its tradition and, most particularly, to his father, his personality and his outlook. These bonds held him firmly throughout his life and became decisive for his problematic relationship to both his surroundings and his own psychic world. In spite of all his critical insights, liberation from these bonds never became possible.

2. From the earliest moment he was brought up in close connection with a disturbed father whose suffering permanently marked Kierkegaard's mind, which from the start was shocked by the impressions it suffered.

3. By nature Kierkegaard was equipped with very unusual abilities for abstract thinking, with a unique talent for language, and with a magnificently virtuoso literary imagination. These qualities put him in a special class as a superior personality, not as a psychically deviant person.

4. From earliest childhood and throughout his life, his temperament and basic disposition was marked by a kind of psycho-insufficiency, an inability to establish himself among other people as an unusually gifted person in their midst. This failing was to a certain extent innate but it was also reinforced to an extreme degree by the shocks already mentioned. These gave his mind that mood that he himself called (in a terminologically misleading way) his melancholy. As a mood it was related to his ability with language and to the aesthetic elements in his personality. This mood remained as a constant feature throughout his whole life, *without fluctuation*; it was an expression of his innermost self, maintained throughout all the dramatic conflicts of his life, and recognizable in all his writings from first to last.

5. Kierkegaard's life was filled with tensions all of which are explicable in terms of the tension between the Kierkegaardian nature (the family atmosphere) and the environment, the tension regarding his purpose in life—whether he should become an aesthetic, philosophical or religious writer—and the tension between his own social poverty and his desire to realize himself in community life. All these tensions remained unresolved and became the source of the energy behind his enormous literary activity. They may be seen everywhere as the driving force of his work.

6. Over the years, his psycho-insufficiency was reinforced by a *social sensitivity*, nourished by the disproportion between his gifts and his ability to act, and finally established as a fact by his perception of himself as the individual, the exception, the sacrificed.

It was not as "a genius in a market town" but as a transformed symbol of his personal difficulties that he became the (chosen) one among the many.

7. There is *one psychologically normal and understandable line* running through Kierkegaard's entire life. The threads lie side by side all the way from the radical experiences of his childhood to the final eruption. This eruption illustrates all the problems in a violent discovery in which every consideration is thrust aside in order to break the tensions which had been accumulating. The explosion could be termed abnormal because Kierkegaard, no longer able to control his inner problems as he once had, exposed them before all and sundry. But it could also be termed an extremely normal reaction if viewed as the final definitive attempt to come out of his confinement, which unquestionably demanded an unusual amount of passion and unaccustomed activity.

8. All these fundamental phenomena and mental processes are in strict accordance with the concrete life that Kierkegaard led both as a man and as a literary personality. They explain why he became the man he did and it is impossible to overemphasize the fact that no further pathological relationships are required by way of explanation. *It is impossible to find manic-depressive features* in his writings, journals, or even his biography. One finds in these sources a constancy and consistency which is entirely explicable by normal psychological methods and which leaves no room for the unintelligible intrusion of endogenous (hereditary) fluctuations of the mind. The only two factors to which psycho-pathology may have contributed are his psycho-insufficiency and its reinforcement of his social sensitivity and, with some reservations, the final expansive phase. But these also are closely connected with the circumstances under which Kierkegaard grew up and lived. These conditions and the lighter, more intelligible and more easily sensed psychopathological components illuminate each other beautifully. It is true that Kierkegaard's family was burdened with a manic-depressive predisposition. But one cannot conclude from this that Søren Kierkegaard also suffered this characteristic. In a large family such as his it is possible for an individual to be inclined toward illness while the others go free.

When Hjalmar Helweg's psychiatric work on Kierkegaard[9] was published (Copenhagen, 1933) I accepted it as an extremely thorough

---

[9] Hjalmar Helweg, *Søren Kierkegaard. En psykiatrisk-psykologisk studie.* The views discussed here are found throughout this book.

and skilful work and I dared not openly challenge its conclusions at
that time. By coincidence I published, in the same year, my study on
*The Concept of Dread* in which I suggested some views on Kierkegaard's illness that were different from Helweg's but, though never
really satisfied with his book, I felt at the time that I did not have
sufficient experience to present an alternative to it. Now, however,
although I may not have worked through the whole corpus of Kierkegaard's writings as Helweg did, I think that I have studied most of it
through the years. I have been virtually imprisoned by Kierkegaard's
life and thoughts, have been unable to free myself from them, and
they have continually influenced my psychological thinking. What I
may lack in scholarly learning is, in my opinion, fully counter-
balanced by a long shared life with this amazing and unhappy man. I
have held many silent discussions with him while sitting in my room
listening to his monologues, be they philosophically existential,
aesthetic, or inwardly religious. The years have also given me a
clearer psychiatric view so that I now feel qualified to oppose Helweg's views with reasons that forty years ago were only partially
developed.

I can still agree with Frithiof Brandt[10] the professor of philosophy
who, in addition to some rather critical remarks, wrote at the end of
his review (*Doctor's Weekly*, June 1934) that Helweg's book "contains
a wealth of normal psychological analyses that will benefit
Kierkegaard scholars." Helweg was a distinguished psychiatric writer
but, as the reader may have discovered, my understanding of
Kierkegaard is very different from his. It seems to me that the foundation of Helweg's study is in conflict with the two basic principles of
pathographic evaluation that I mentioned at the beginning of this
chapter. His purpose was to show that Kierkegaard was a psychiatric
case by deliberate diagnosis and he attempted to understand Kierkegaard's life and literary production as the consequence of this
suffering. In Helweg's hand Kierkegaard becomes a psychiatric pa-
tient who became the intellectual figure that he was because of his
pathological predisposition. In my opinion, this is not a particularly
helpful point of view as it does not contribute to a greater understanding of Kierkegaard's actual work or, especially, its form. It
seems very strange that Helweg did not pause to consider Kierkegaard as a genius, as an exceptional man, with the peculiarities and

---

[10] Brandt was a Danish philosopher born in 1891.

the psychological problems which this created. He goes so far as to suggest that if Kierkegaard had not suffered manic-depressive psychosis there would have been no Søren Kierkegaard—no literary phenomenon corresponding to this famous name. This is a very surprising idea and one that really ignores what we have explained above about the psychology of genius.

Helweg's opinions may be refuted point by point.

1. He states that Kierkegaard suffered from a chronic manic-depressive psychosis in which depressive, manic and mixed phases replaced each other in sequence. My reply to this is that there is nothing in either the writings or his biography that proves this diagnosis. The description of the mixed phases, which are always extremely difficult to demonstrate in a person who lived more than a hundred years ago, are based on intelligent constructions rather than on convincing material. Helweg was preoccupied with these forms of psychosis and in clinical cases he could often demonstrate certain aspects of this type of psychosis even though such psychosis was not suggested by overt behaviour. In Kierkegaard's case this preoccupation led him to a mistaken interpretation.

2. Kierkegaard's most fruitful periods as a writer are interpreted as manic evolutions. But they were all expressions of his linguistic genius. Furthermore, all literary personalities are subject to a normal rhythm with fluctuations in their productive capacity. Surging and slack periods alternate with each other. Changing problems and their clarification are the condition of all important intellectual work.

3. Kierkegaard's increasing isolation and his movement toward the choice of the category of the individual is viewed as symptomatic of depressive attitudes and their consequences. This is not correct either. Both had the same origin and became synonyms for the attitude toward which his development necessarily and logically led him. In fact, it was a result of his own early glimpsed psycho-insufficiency, combined with the fatal impressions to which he had been exposed in his childhood.

4. The Church struggle is seen as a manic eruption of a particular kind. My reply is that it was an extravagantly displayed consequence of his whole preceding life with its tensions and problems, just as in the preceding literary periods it was a transformation of the conflicts within his personality which he had to solve. On this point Helweg was on the right track in interpreting the massive attack on women, matrimony, the clergy, the church and society as a "revenge toward

the vainly desired." This was precisely the case. But why then resort to further artificial attempts at an explanation by making this "revenge" an expression of mania? It would have been better to replace the word "revenge" with "desperate attempt at rehabilitation."

5. In spite of his extreme diligence and vigilance Helweg did not take sufficient consideration of the natural causes for Kierkegaard's reactions. Earlier in this writing we mentioned examples of concrete events that aroused Kierkegaard's sudden feelings, such as "the indescribable joy." F. Brandt mentions in his review a similar example involving the Danish poet H. Hertz. Pathological interpretations must always be the last explanation, never the first.

6. Finally it is rather strange that Helweg does not distinguish between sexuality and erotic feeling (love) in Kierkegaard. In *The Concept of Dread* Kierkegaard clearly stated that he regarded sexuality as "the not sinful" and that it was his father's case that had forced him to take this view. But elsewhere Kierkegaard is concerned with the erotic and here he was most careful not to confuse the categories and not to reveal anything about the particular phenomenon of sexuality in himself. For Kierkegaard, the problem of personality was everything and Helweg's statement that he was sexually normal seems therefore a little irrelevant and even incompatible with the fact that Kierkegaard's works deal from first to last with matters belonging wholly to the world of ideas.

7. Helweg admits that Kierkegaard had "schizoid" features. This sounds like a polite concession to the critics of his book who may have thought that his awkwardness and psychic isolation had a psychiatric explanation. In my judgement there are no features of this kind in Kierkegaard. Against this loose assumption with its suggestion of a weak self, I would cite Kierkegaard's firm and unchanging self-consciousness together with his self-assurance which, over the years, developed into self-esteem and, eventually, into an overestimation of the self and his rights above those of others. Also I would point as well to his unchanging but inhibited desire for social contact.

Kierkegaard was free of his family's manic-depressive features, including even their slightest traces. They bypassed him as they often bypass other members of a manic-depressive family. All the events of his life are joined by normal psychological lines and they are all intelligible. Likewise, his work follows a clear and straightforward line which shows itself clearly without break or interruption. He is consistent throughout, expressing his own peculiar character in the given circumstances, whether internal and external. He remained himself through all the dramatic changes and realized his personality in all of the ways open to him.

Since its views differ from those of Hj. Helweg, one can antici-pate that this study will be met with the usual triumphant objection that, since the psychiatrists disagree, we need not take their opinions seriously and may even disregard them as strange and rather useless speculation about the composition of great personalities. But the obvious psychological problems cannot be dismissed so easily. Here also, as with all scientific questions subject to the laws of progress, yet more penetrating discussions will, through thesis and antithesis, bring us yet nearer to the truth.

In Kierkegaard's case, one must distinguish between different psycho-medical viewpoints that are of unequal value as tools for the understanding of his life and work. By pathographical investigation one may demonstrate that these have been exclusively or at least predominantly due to psychotic mechanisms. In that case, one is dealing with a biological determinant outside of the normal personal-ity. It may disturb, inhibit or at times even direct what the person thinks, but as a factor standing outside the personality it cannot have a definitely causal relation to what the creating mind wishes to express. Regardless of the barriers created by illness, in such circumstances the pathological factor becomes more or less incidental, in much the same way as it would be if, for example, it were discovered that Kierkegaard suffered from tuberculosis. Of course, it must be recog-nized that in the area of psychology all findings have a certain profes-sional interest.

This survey of the subject covers Helweg's interpretation.

But there are other pathographic investigations where one is accidentally more favourably placed and this is precisely the case with Kierkegaard. Here the pathograph and the human object in its entirety are in the same place, in the engine room as one might say, where both the creating power and the peculiar complicating forces are at work. It then becomes an analysis of the personality seen from different angles but always with the same object—the personality itself in all its distinctive peculiarity. Here one is always within the realm of the intelligible and, in spite of all the serious conflicts and difficulties within the personality, the pathograph is always able to reach its core. The work of the pathographer can go hand in hand with literary and normal psychological analyses and his particular viewpoint can contribute significantly to the understanding of Kierkegaard's mind. Psychiatrically speaking, Kierkegaard was what one might call a borderline case in the sense that he had a firm grip on the course of events as seen both subjectively (from his own perspective) and objectively. There was no phasic phenomena that would commute or reverse the development that was in progress (as was the case with Grundtvig, in respect to whom Helweg is absolutely right).

The results of Helweg's pathographic investigation are consistent with the present small treatise. This agreement is important from the point of view of showing how the understanding can be enriched by combining normal (though rather unusual) features with others which are peculiar and tending toward the abnormal, and doing this in such a way as to illuminate each other and to reach a higher synthesis. It is not the case that the psychiatrists disagree, but that two investigators, each with his own methods and his own opinion of what is objectively true, have reached two different conclusions. In my own opinion, my conclusion is more valuable because it leads into the life of Kierkegaard but this assertion should not be misunderstood. It is bound up with the fact that my approach assumes that Kierkegaard is a normal person conditioned by his circumstances. Between Helweg and myself there is real disagreement but no contradiction, as the famous Danish psychiatrist Knud Pontoppidan has expressed elsewhere about such diverging opinions.

I owe Kierkegaard a great deal. The drama of his life continues to attract me and the noble way in which he tries to come to terms with his unhappy conditions binds me to him and to his sombre family tradition. His life was one long and private struggle against the demons in his heart and in his brain, but his mind did not allow itself to be intimidated. It changed all tragedy and despair into inwardness and confidence by means of that strength which he never doubted and by which he gave voice to a profoundly sublime tangle of thoughts covered with those exuberant decorations of his rich language which, in his loneliness, he produced in such rich variety. The language and the pen became his closest friends, his last resort and the firm foundation of his inwardness.

There is nothing constructed or even particularly unusual in the version of Kierkegaard's life I have presented in these pages. It is the old story of *the late revision* of unhappy childhood experiences and the necessarily critical settlement of his father's offences, in the form of reflection or inwardness. The fugitive crosses the old tracks and discovers how his life was planned from the beginning—so disastrously, so irretrievably. Indignation, pity and reconciliation struggle in his mind and he feels himself in the power of destiny. But for Kierkegaard destiny was not to have the last word. If it comes to that, it was not Kierkegaard's life that was exceptional; it was Kierkegaard himself, his mind and his genius. That is the point where we must stop. Beyond it we can go no further.

# 10

# The Fundamental Impulse behind Kierkegaard's Authorship

I

It is a striking fact that the two most important religious personalities in Danish intellectual life, Grundtvig and Kierkegaard, had to come to terms with the same central problem, *viz.*, the question of finding a guarantee of the truth of Christianity. Each found this guarantee for himself from two diametrically opposed sources, the outward and the inward.

Grundtvig put the question as one of "true Christianity and the truth of Christianity" and he found its solution in the continued existence through the ages of the congregation and its accompanying sacraments and words.

Kierkegaard looked inwards and found his solution in a state of mind, in a sincere and paradoxical faith of the individual which, in spite of all reason, confirmed what Christ had from earliest times demanded of his followers. For Kierkegaard there could be no greater security than this constantly renewed faith in the truth which reveals itself only to inwardness, that inwardness which bridges the absurdities of life.

Complicated man that he was, Kierkegaard was unable to accept the orthodoxy of his family. His authorship thus became one long argument for a Christian point of view based on his own mind's innermost point of support where thought and feeling could meet and become one. On the other hand, he could not conceive his own life outside the Christianity of his family.

One quite decisive and moving reason for this was the terrifying experience of his aged father's distressing doubt regarding the authenticity of his Christian faith, a doubt which was itself caused by the old man's heavy, depressive moods. The father's case illustrated for the son the classical crisis between intellectual doubt and personal faith and with deep reverence Kierkegaard took his father's problem as the subject of his own writing. This is clear from the disguised story (in *Concluding Unscientific Postscript*, pp. 212f.) about the old man and his grandchild in the churchyard which he describes as "the most moving scene I had ever witnessed."

Surely this story represents exactly what Kierkegaard had experienced with the wool trader. It shows him that "modern speculation, like a change of currency, has made property values in the realm of faith insecure" (ibid., p. 216). Then he understands that he should devote his life as a writer to this problem: "to discover where the misunderstanding lies between speculation and Christianity" (ibid., p. 216). He continues, "My principal thought was that in our age, because of the great increase of knowledge, we had forgotten what it means to *exist*, and what *inwardness* signifies, and that the misunderstanding between speculative philosophy and Christianity was explicable on that ground. I now resolved to go back as far as possible..." (ibid., p. 223) in order to disentangle the ground of this dubious relation.

He began with *Either/Or* which is not only a magnificent introduction to the authorship, but also the first argument in the debate. His mission in life was given by his father's temptations which set the son's thoughts soaring from the start. He wished to come to the assistance of his dead father and to ease his agony and thereafter his own philosophical needs drove him on to the completion of his work. The problem had been posed for him, *viz.*, the absolute difference between mere thinking (speculation) and being, between exact knowledge and concrete being as an existing individual, between impersonal and personal life.

Kierkegaard's original interest in the question "What is it to exist?" was not rooted in harrowing personal experiences in his own life, as is the case with some modern existentialists. One thinks, for example, of Heidegger who, during the war, directly experienced with terrifying reality the opposition between life and death, being and non-being. By contrast, Kierkegaard's interest in this question originated characteristically in an internal family matter which he subsequently extended into a general philosophical question.

An incident between Kierkegaard and Sibbern to which he himself refers in the *Papers* indicates how much Kierkegaard was concerned with these thoughts. Before he had started writing he met the friendly professor of philosophy on the Gammeltorv and immediately asked him about the relationship between philosophy and real life. The question "surprised" Sibbern by its impulsiveness but later he saw that it was a natural one for a thinker who was still concerned with Hegel, since the Hegelians never studied philosophy existentially. Even at this early time then, Kierkegaard was already quietly on the attack against this German thinker who was virtually supreme at that time.

Some people have thought Kierkegaard's production to be too widely dispersed with too many points of departure and too many widely different fields of interest. But the opposite is the case; in fact, it is extremely homogeneous. Like many other great literary personalities, he had only one major idea that he wanted to establish and to present in as many variations as possible. That idea was that every man is a being in himself and that this can never be established as a truth by philosophical speculation, but only in terms of the personality itself, through the inwardness and passion of faith. This homogeneity in the foundation of the entire production has never been fully recognized since it is often hidden by a wealth of details. Kierkegaard himself emphasized this in his survey of the literature produced between 1843 and 1846 which he included in the *Concluding Unscientific Postscript* and of which this work is itself the climax. What followed thereafter were only further modulations on the theme presented in his first book. This may be seen from the fact that the Kierkegaardian key-words "existence," "paradox," "despair," "dread," and "leap" are all used from the beginning, nourished throughout, and presented in new ways in the later works.

Rather than a series of abrupt developments, his production as a writer could instead be seen as a continuum of intricate variations and fugues on the basic theme that had set him working in the first place. His constant question is what it is to exist and this he presents now in direct and now in indirect form. This presentation is illustrated by a gallery of fictitious characters: those who live without existing in the personal sense; the many who both will and will not to exist (and consequently suffer all kinds of trials); and the few who really do exist affirming their concrete personal existence with all its contrasts and contradictions. He is like Bach who sits at his organ and plays one theme through in every key.

Using his instrument of language, Kierkegaard improvised on the theme that his father had given him. The prelude was firm. The basic idea was maintained both within each individual work and from one work to another throughout his short, intense life as a writer. How have people been able to believe in the face of these facts that he was ill? This is contradicted by the fact that the hallmark of his authorship is his consistency and his ability to vary in an almost infinite multitude of ways the task which he performed. His intense production had but one single purpose, *viz.*, to convince the reader that his father's case was justified. His father had been put through the trials of personal existence and was directed against the full recognition of truth by his scruples toward religious interpretation. For the son, this was the only way to escape both the painful contradictions of existence and the fantastic and imaginary pictures of speculative philosophy.

It is strange to see this eminent thinker employing all his dialectical energy as an anti-thinker. His principal work is called "unscientific." This is not a mere gesture but is rather his definitive refusal of speculative in favour of existential thinking with respect to all essentially human matters.

Piety, recast into a philosophical problem, was the driving force behind his work. But it was not some personal crisis. He was destined to remain a Kierkegaard, but in his own way. He reached beyond the orthodoxy of his family and at last he broke with it, still, no doubt, with the secret thought that in this he had his father on his side. Here was one of the few righteous ones who knew the pain of existence— and the cure for it in the religious.

Kierkegaard's impressive discussion of the relation of the erotic and the sexual (in *The Concept of Dread*, 1844) is surely connected with his well known experiences in his own home and with his relation to Regine. But this must not be misunderstood: Kierkegaard was not a crypto-erotic author. On the contrary, he sees the erotic as something which can even prevent the spirit from ruling the soul.

## II

The whole of Kierkegaard's philosophy of existence and his fight against speculative philosophy is aimed at promoting a religious interpretation of existence. It is the firm foundation of all his aesthetic and ethical works. He was much more richly equipped than the other members of his family with aesthetic and philosophical abilities and he had to fight with himself to defend his Kierkegaardian emphasis that only in religious inwardness and in piously confessing the paradoxical contradictions of personal life was it possible to grasp the truth.

He knew that one could choose the easier way of becoming a speculative mind but he also knew that this would mean abstracting the mind from life and changing it into an objective problem without considering that it is also itself in existence. For such a mind thinking and being become the same thing, but at the same time it remains outside the life which it tries to understand. The speculative mind will even defend Christianity by thinking, but it can never do more than indicate possibilities. For Kierkegaard, this was ridiculous. (Here he is in opposition to Pascal who wanted to show the truth of Christianity by his scientific mind.) The speculative mind does not see that "this collision of finite and infinite . . . is precisely a mortal danger for him who is a composite of both" (*Postscript*, p. 208). Nor does it see that the existing spirit must grasp both every instant of his life. "All (merely theoretical) knowledge about reality is possibility. The only reality to which an existing individual may have a relation that is more than cognitive, is his own reality, the fact that he exists . . ." (ibid., p. 280). But by this the existing individual is painfully forced to recognize in himself an ineradicable opposition between understanding life abstractly and living life concretely. For him, thinking and being are widely different things. The existing individual chooses the difficult path of taking up his concrete existence. He realizes that every person is a subject, with his destiny in his own hands; in spite of the contradictions of life he feels within himself, he realizes that he must live concretely in the present, that he must constantly develop, that he is not permitted to formalize his thoughts about life in a philosophical system. His life must never stagnate but always move forward in the categories of decision, determination, and repetition; categories which exist only for the subjective personality. He does not evade the difficult confrontation with the fact that one must take responsibility for his life in time and eternity, that one must contemplate life deeply and thus make thinking and being one. He also recognizes that man is a contradictory composition of the eternal and the temporal. The eternal in man is definitely not the same as concrete eternity, which is a religious category; rather, it is the passionate anticipation of the eternal and thus the closest approximation possible for a temporal individual.

The decisive difference between the existing spirit and the merely speculating individual is that the former acknowledges the paradoxes of life. For the paradox between the temporal and the eternal component in the human mind, Kierkegaard uses the completely Platonic image of the cart and driver: "... if someone hitched a team of horses to a wagon for him, one of them a Pegasus and the other a worn-out jade, and told him to drive .... And it is just this that it means to exist, if one is to become conscious of it. Eternity is the winged-horse, infinitely fast, and time is a worn-out jade; the existing individual is the driver ..." (ibid., p. 276).

But does it follow that one can overcome the paradoxes and thus live with the existential contradictions within oneself and realize one's given subjectivity? This can happen but only when the single individual "in the moment of decision," with divine aid, grasps faith in inwardness by an absurd leap. The individual must maintain the fundamental uncertainty in the passion of faith—which passion is to be understood not as intense feeling but as the closest possible relationship to this unintelligible existence into which we are cast. The paradox must not be wrongly understood; to the reason it is the absurd and can only be maintained through the inwardness of faith. This is the limit put by God for the relationship between the existing individual and the eternal truth. It is a category just as valid as the other categories of reason and it needs no further explanation. Indeed, for Kierkegaard there was even an "unspeakable joy" in the paradox, a "divine breath" in one who is willing to recognize God as God and man as just man. Inwardness accepts the paradox as a winged accomplice with whose help it rises to faith. Spiritually, faith and inwardness are the same, inwardness being an organ for the recognition of the truth which can only be experienced in the light of faith. Like the paradox it is a category of the understanding, "the seriousness of the absurd." These ideas are related to Indian philosophy: the "self" which views the contradictions of the human *I* is not a new human self but the God, Brahma.

Kierkegaard begins and ends with the maxim that only religious truth is truth. And since religious truth can only be perceived through inwardness in the individual, the philosophical result is the famous statement that subjectivity is truth. He who does not opt for the religious through inwardness falls under the category of sin, which is non-faith. But men try all possible ways of avoiding or postponing this leap into the presence of the eternal. All of Kierkegaard's pseudonyms and fictitious characters illustrate the many ways in which men become anxious about and seek to evade this one necessary step. All these attitudes are really despair because eternity does not let itself be fooled but forever stands by with its claim and its offer, no matter how people try to escape it.

Is there not, in spite of its philosophical guise, some small human offence in Kierkegaard's idea? Are there really many people with much self-understanding who have not at some time or other felt a sombre warning within themselves of the almost grotesque incomprehensibility of personal existence? And does this not happen despite the fact that, as natural subjects of the world, they also succeed in living in the concrete reality which surrounds them and occupies them as the most important thing?

An example of this universal duplicity has been given by Georg Brandes in his memorial book about his friend Julius Lange. The situation stems, no doubt, from a walk the two friends took to the island of Møen. Brandes writes: "We were (that was in 1862) both equally convinced of the infinity of the self and therefore understood each other perfectly on the really fundamental views. I stood beside a chair and asked Lange if he felt it as mad as I, that I, this infinity, was also thus something finite, that this chair and I were two objects. No thought is more familiar to me, he answered; how ridiculous is the idea that I who span time and space find myself half a mile from [the country town] Præstø."

If Kierkegaard had known of this episode, he would have smiled knowingly at the two young men and answered: "My young gentlemen, you have just faced the paradox, flanked as it is by the Cerberus of dread and despair. Or let me as a work of love tell you that your deepest longings have moved your minds as the flutter of the wings of eternity. But you turned away in doubt and did not even reach the point that I have called Religiousness A; you chose this side and let the gate stay bolted. But I know better. You are two of my pseudonyms and they do not go my way but lead astray. However, I wish you luck on your journey and take care at the next crossing . . . ."

The last link in Kierkegaard's chain of thought is the claim that Christianity meets the contradictions in the human not by being a teaching, which demands understanding, but by being an existence-communication. It is the lynch pin for his view of existence, a proof even to him of its certainty. It is founded upon the existential paradox that the eternal developed in historical time and that it cannot be understood through speculation but only by the individual who, in defiance of the offence of reason and through "despair," can reach faith in subjective inwardness. Inwardness is the only means of bridging over the chasm of the paradox. Only when man accepts his existential situation, finds himself out over 70,000 fathoms, and yet longs to choose himself decisively, has he met the condition for recognizing the eternal truth which comes to him only in Christianity. It accentuates the existential situation, being as a paradox, and release from this paradox through recognizing oneself as a sinner, as one who in his natural state is a non-believer but who only has to grasp faith in religious inwardness through Religiousness B. Faith alone presents the truth to the individual. Truth can only be reached along the religious way, but when that happens "the struggle suddenly disappears."

Put briefly: What the natural man experiences in a real way as the unintelligibility of his existence and the demand of the eternal for a place within him and as his own distance from this eternal which incessantly "censures" him in order that he might grasp it through the leap of decision—with all this does Christianity approach man. It refuses speculation as a way to the truth; it addresses itself to the individual and invites the sincere dedication of faith including the (incomprehensible) sufferings of the paradox which is one with inwardness; and it identifies all ways of life which avoid the decision of faith as sin. Since religiousness is the only way to understand the truth, sin is defined as departing from the truth.

In this way the question of whether Kierkegaard was an aesthetical, philosophical or religious writer solves itself: he was from beginning to end a religious writer. The whole of his writing after *Concluding Unscientific Postscript* is a continuous depth analysis of the nature of Christianity as he experienced it. *Sickness Unto Death* describes the ways in which man avoids the eternal—the spirit—and chooses despair. *Training in Christianity* emphasizes the severity and offence of Christianity and, conversely, what imitation of and contemporaneity with Christ must mean. *Works of Love* is a profound analysis or philosophical sermon concerning the proper Christian life.

An analysis of Kierkegaard's production shows that in contrast to his family, he reached the view that truth—and with that faith—is a state of mind and that this state of mind is congruous with the demands of Christianity. With his very free relationship to the evangelical tradition, he was able both to support his father in his doubt by emphasizing the religious attitude, regardless of the opinions of the individual, and to find his own standpoint, consistent with his philosophical doubts. It has also been shown that Kierkegaard's original preoccupation with the problem of existence was not based upon personal catastrophes but on his desire to assist his father and other tempted souls in facing the doubts that speculation (especially Hegelianism) had raised. Finally, analysis shows that Kierkegaard's authorship, in spite of its labyrinthine structure, is extremely consistent, with a constant theme from beginning to end. That he finally became desperate is understandable when we consider his isolated position. He held a new and unusual interpretation of Christianity and, with that, of existence, an interpretation that was contrary to the spirit and the major personalities of the time. Since no one would understand his message (which was really the message of all the Kierkegaards) he was forced to use extreme means. These were against his nature and fragile constitution and are the real source of the unrestrained and the fanatical character of the final struggle, the power of which sprang from his violent duplicity: to be faithful to his father and, at the same time, to go beyond him.

The views expressed in H. S. Vodskov's valuable investigation *An Episode in S. Kierkegaard's Life*[11] (published in 1884) are completely consistent with the explanation presented here. Using the papers that had then just been published, Vodskov proved that Kierkegaard's inner problem—whether he should be satisfied to remain a religious writer and poet or whether he should draw the consequences of his own authorship to date and step into character as a reformer and polemical defender of original Christianity—forced him to his mental limit during the years 1849-1853. The latter of these alternatives prevailed and, characteristically, it was because he could not get his father out of this thoughts. He could not fail him. His sufferings demanded that he sacrifice the very attractive compromise of being a mere poet and become instead a follower of Christ. In the eyes of his dead father, such a compromise would have been "to defraud truth and to mock God." It would have been "to abuse the holy," to

---

[11] This piece appears in Vodskov's *Spredte Studier* [Scattered Letters] (Copenhagen, 1884), pp. 1-30.

choose dishonesty before honesty. He must follow his road to the bitter end. "The memories of the past," Vodskov writes, "were forced to the surface . . . the impressions he received from the tales of his father's suffering haunted him, and he was constantly obsessed with the idea that Christ was spat upon."

In this choice of struggle instead of poetry Kierkegaard actually transcended his psychical and physical limits and finally caused his exalted lack of balance. But even this still shows as clearly as possible the coherence of his life and personality as a writer. Vodskov hides nothing when he describes the alarming symptoms of Kierkegaard's abnormal reactions—his distrustfulness, his wrongdoing, his bitterness and, not least of all, his extreme feelings of pride and self-admiration.

In this respect, I have certainly been more lenient in my judgement, but on the other hand Vodskov's penetrating analysis shows that I have been on the right track and that I have in him a strong supporter. Religious humility and an inverately ironical self-esteem remained as the two poles around which Kierkegaard's mental life revolved.

It is impossible to avoid the thought that Kierkegaard's teachings on existence anticipated the problems of modern physics. In 1929 Niels Bohr wrote that in atomic theory "no sharp distinction between object and subject can be maintained" in the face of the so-called objective content of thought, and that "strictly speaking, the conscious (objective) analysis of any notion stands in a relationship of exclusion to its immediate (subjective) application." In accordance with Bohr's analogical psychological parallels, this must also apply to thoughts about the deepest foundations of existence. Not even here can subjectivity ultimately be detached from the final constructions of our thought since existence is constantly being applied as a subjective starting point in our speculative formulations. Subjectivity is a part of the truth.

# Appendix

There were two men in whom Kierkegaard had unaltered confidence through the many years in which he knew them and until the day he died. They were Hans Brøchner[12] and Emil Boesen.[13] What preserved his warm sympathy was the deep honesty of the two friends and their striving—each in his own way—after personal truth. Neither of them sought outward honours but were motivated by a self-effacing aspiration which is one with quiet piety before the mystery of life. Their quiet gentleness attracted Kierkegaard who could relax in their company, free from all controversy. They were to him as a solace from the constant struggle, a healing salve on an open wound. Kierkegaard's search for inwardness in others found its goal in them as he himself continued to cling to inwardness in spite of all the struggle and strife. Religious inwardness was his anchorage through every storm and when he found an echo of this feeling in another individual he was able to relax his vigilance. His friends helped him stay alive and his warm affection for Brøchner and Boesen indicate that even in the middle of his slightly disturbed behaviour he could still maintain the balance of his being. This does not invalidate what was described above as his fanatical social struggle with its unveiling of many private conflicts.

---

[12] Hans Brøchner (1820-1875) was a Danish philosopher.

[13] Emil Boesen (1812-1881) was a clergyman and long-time friend of Kierkegaard.

On December 2, 1855, shortly after Kierkegaard's death, Brøchner wrote his friend Chr. K. F. Molbech (as part of their considerable correspondence edited in 1902 by H. Høffding): "It is with pleasure that I think of all the years that I have known him, almost twenty years, and how that mild and loving part of his nature constantly asserted itself over the highly ironical and polemical element which was in him by nature; and how his thought continually became richer, deeper and clearer, so that a word from him could have a reassuring and reconciling effect and could resolve a confusion that you could not yourself come to terms with." In the same letter Brøchner admits that Kierkegaard "has meant very much to me, both in his writings and in the personal relationship which I have had with him"—until the last difficult year. In a later letter (February 17, 1856) Brøchner states explicitly: "I knew that in this last difficult struggle, when 'his wish was for death, his longing for the grave and his desire was that this wish and this longing would soon be fulfilled,' he maintained his loving compassion for others even in the smallest matters in life; he still kept the gentleness, the kindness, even the jokes; kept a balance of mind and a clarity of thought and, above all, he maintained peace and repose in the faith that did not leave him, not even in the severe pain of his deathbed" (cf. *Dru*, p. 553).

This beautiful testimony, together with Boesen's touching loyalty, do not alter the views that have been presented in this work concerning the psychological mechanisms that ruled Kierkegaard during the struggle with the Church. Rather, they confirm the religious inwardness that sustained his psychic balance in the midst of that explosive reaction, serving as the firm and invulnerable core of his mind that could not be attacked. The foundations of the fortress were shaken but the innermost tower itself did not budge. His confidence was forever rooted in the Kierkegaardian motto: alone with God. With that in his heart the outer struggle was "as good as gone" and in taking leave of life he could look forward "to rest myself in rosy valleys and there speak eternally with my Jesus."

What the two friends testify to so beautifully, and what they declare to posterity, is that all the internal and external strife that Kierkegaard had to live through from the cradle to the grave was nevertheless unable to penetrate to the core of his mind. Here was a sacred spot, the bright and fresh oasis of his mind, untouched by the storms of his life, the impregnable sanctuary of his gentleness and his inner joy. There were two doors to his mind. One led outward to